Venison Cookbook

0 11557 02594 1

VENISON COOKBOOK

A. D. Livingston

STACKPOLE
BOOKS

Published by
STACKPOLE BOOKS
5067 Ritter Road
Mechanicsburg, PA 17055

Cover illustration and design by Mark B. Olszewski
Interior design by Nick Gregoric

Printed in the United States of America

First Edition

10 9 8 7 6

Other Books by A. D. Livingston: *Outdoor Life's Complete Fish & Game
Cookbook; Good Vittles; Cast-Iron Cooking; Grilling, Smoking, and Barbecuing;
Edible Plants and Animals (with Dr. Helen N. Livingston)*

Library of Congress Cataloging-in-Publication Data

Livingston, A. D., 1932–
     Venison cookbook / A.D. Livingston.—1st ed.
        p.   cm.
     Includes index.
     ISBN 0-8117-2594-4 (pb) :
     1. Cookery (Venison)   2. Low-fat diet—Recipes.   I. Title.
TX751.L59   1993
641.6'91—dc20

                                                                    93-4400
                                                                    CIP

CONTENTS

ACKNOWLEDGMENTS

The author would like to acknowledge recipes adapted from *The Art of American Indian Cooking* by Yeffe Kimball and Jean Anderson, copyright 1965, reprinted by permission of McIntosh and Otis, Inc.; material from the author's article "Don't Stew over Venison," reprinted courtesy of *Southern Outdoors Magazine* and B.A.S.S. Inc.; material from *The Official Louisiana Seafood & Wild Game Cookbook*, reprinted with permission from the State of Louisiana Department of Wildlife and Fisheries; brief quotations from *The Complete Book of Outdoor Cookery* by James A. Beard and Helen Evans Brown, reprinted by permission of HarperCollins Publishers; a recipe reprinted from *Alaska Magazine's Cabin Cookbook* by permission of *Alaska* magazine; a recipe from *Cracklin Bread and Asfidity: Folk Recipes and Remedies*, compiled by Jack and Olivia Solomon, copyright 1979, used by permission of the University of Alabama Press; a recipe from *The Maine Way*, published by the Maine Department of Inland Fisheries and Wildlife; material from *Wildlife Cookbook*, published by the North Carolina Wildlife Resources Commission; and a recipe from *Cooking the Sportsman's Harvest II*, published by the South Dakota Department of Game, Fish, and Parks.

INTRODUCTION

The word *venison* usually refers to the edible flesh of deer and similar animals, such as elk, moose, and caribou. Although most of the recipes in this book can be used with any good venison, the white-tailed deer predominates the text simply because it is by far the most plentiful and popular big-game animal in North America. It's also one of the best for eating.

I may have stuck my neck out concerning the organization of this book. It would have been safer, from a writer's viewpoint, to start at the beginning and go through the rather gory details of field dressing, butchering, and so on in chapter 1. I feel, however, that many modern hunters haul their deer to a local meat processor for butchering and would therefore tend to skip over some of the material. Also, many people buy ranch-raised or market venison of one sort or another and would have no use for a section on butchery. For these reasons I have put some of this material in an appendix called "Ten Steps Toward Better Venison."

Nevertheless, I must emphasize that any chef worth his salt ought to be familiar with the various cuts of venison and should be able to tell the meat processor what he wants and how he wants it. I might add that my conclusions regarding how a deer or other animal should be reduced to usable parts and cooked are vastly different from—and may be at odds with—the accepted practices and recommendations in other books. For example, many recipes in other books call for "larding" the meat with a "larding needle." Well, who has a larding needle these days? Where can you buy one? Even if you find one, do you want to lace your lean venison with strips of beef suet or hog fat?

Another example: Most meat processors will add a considerable amount of beef suet or pork fat to ground venison, calling the results "gameburger." Further, many hunters who process their own meat will add beef suet or pork fat simply because many books and magazine articles tell them to do so. In some cases, the fat isn't needed. In other cases, the fat keeps the ground meat from being too dry. My recommendations on these matters are set forth at the beginning of the chapters on ground venison, stew meat, venison cutlets, and so on. Later in the chapters, I get down to recipes.

I must add here that success with venison at the table depends very much on how the animal was killed and handled in the field, no matter who performs the butchering or cooking. I am almost tempted to add a disclaimer here, saying that if the animal isn't cleanly killed and promptly field dressed, then I guarantee nothing. I won't preach about this, but I always start hemming and hawing whenever a hunter offers me a deer or meat from a deer that has been chased all over the country by dogs before the kill—and I become even more evasive, and look for the door, when he asks me to cook it for him. To be perfectly honest, a deer that hasn't been properly handled isn't fit to eat, and there is nothing the chef can do to help it. Marinades can't work magic. The same is true about a sheep or a hog that has been riled up before slaughter. On the other hand, a deer that has been cleanly killed, promptly field dressed, and duly hung can make some wonderful eating if the cook knows his stuff. But it all begins with the hunter—and don't ever forget it.

A. D. Livingston
November 1, 1992

ONE

Venison Steaks, Cutlets, and Chops

The steaks, cutlets, and chops from deer, elk, moose, and other large animals can be compared to familiar cuts of beef and pork. Although the size of the cuts will depend on the size of the animal, such a comparison helps frame a better image of what's what. Always, the best meat—or at least the tenderest—grows along the back, from the neck to the rump. The reason, of course, is that the muscles in the back simply aren't used as much as those in the legs.

The first half of the backbone (the rib section) contains two small but very good strips of meat along the top. This is the same piece of beef that is so popular these days as rib eye steaks. With a meat saw, this section can be cut into chops that contain part of a rib, as in lamb chops. Such chops are certainly feasible cuts for anyone lucky enough to have an elk or moose, but in deer, the chops are quite small. If you butcher your own meat without an electric meat saw, I think it is best to cut out the "eye" and treat it like a tenderloin strip. The rib section of these chops can then be included in the rack of ribs, and the backbone proper can be used in soup.

The loin section, or saddle, refers to the backbone and the attached muscle between the ribs and the rump. It includes loins and the tenderloins. The tenderloins run underneath the backbone, one on either side. These are exposed when the animal is field dressed and should be removed at that time. Leaving them in the animal causes them to dry out and become hard on the outside. Because they can be removed without skinning and butchering the animal, they are popular in deer camp cookery. The tenderloins can be cooked in various ways and are discussed elsewhere in this book as well as in this chapter. For an ordinary whitetail, the tenderloins are small and often butterflied—cut crossways into segments, with each segment then being cut almost in two and folded out. This produces a butterfly-shaped piece of meat. Wrap these pieces in bacon and you have the venison equivalent of filet mignon.

After the animal is skinned, the loins can be cut out from the side of the backbone. These choice muscles are larger than the tenderloins and not quite as tender. The loins can be cut into steaks or chops, and they can be butterflied. They can also be cooked whole as a roast. Sometimes, this piece of meat is cut out with the belly flank meat attached, then rolled and tied as a roast.

Also, the saddle can be left whole and cooked as a roast, or it can be cut with a meat saw into steaks. The backbone can be cut in half lengthwise with a meat saw; then the two halves can be cut into T-bone steaks, similar to those from beef. If the tenderloin is removed in field dressing, then the T-bone will be reduced to a bone-in New York strip steak. Often, the saddle is left whole and sliced crossways into steaks, which are nothing more than two T-bones joined together.

It seems obvious to me that anyone who does his own butchering without an electric meat saw (which can cut the steaks to exact and uniform thicknesses) should consider going for the loins and tenderloins. These cuts contain most of the loin meat and can be removed with a good pocketknife. (What's left of the backbone can be used to great advantage in soups and stews.) Both the loins and the tenderloins, basically cigar-shaped, can be wrapped and frozen whole. Then they may be sliced as needed, or they can be left whole in case you want to cook them that way. Whole pieces keep better and very cold or partly frozen meat is much easier to slice uniformly.

The cuts discussed above are the most tender meat on the deer or any other animal that runs a lot. Steaks can also be cut from the legs, and round steak of venison is almost exactly like that of beef. Of course, there are variations in size, but all of these steaks can be cooked pretty much alike no matter whether they are from whitetail, mule deer, elk, moose, or caribou. The thickness is what matters most during cooking and, with such large steaks, it is almost necessary to have a good electric meat saw to make uniform cuts. Whether you or a processor slices the meat, you should decide how thick you want it. Steaks to be cooked in a skillet should be about ½ inch thick, and steaks to be grilled or broiled should be an inch or more thick. But there are exceptions, and it's difficult to cook a variety of recipes with meat that has been cut to same thickness. That's reason enough for leaving your pieces whole until you are ready to cook.

I suggest that the hunter (or anyone fortunate enough to have good venison) should abandon the round steak concept. Instead, divide the hind legs into oblong pieces. This is easy if you follow the natural division of the muscles, each connected with tough membrane or tissue. Then each segment can be cooked whole as a small roast or sliced into cutlets or chops. These end up looking very much like loin or tenderloin cuts, but they are tougher. Before cooking these cuts, consider marinating or using a commercial tenderizer, or pounding the pieces with a meat mallet or the edge of a plate.

So there you have it, the best ways to reduce a deer to choice cuts of meat at home or at the meat processing plant. It is possible to get "steaks" from flank or shoulder meat, but these are, in my opinion, best used as stew meat or in shoulder roasts.

SLOW-AND-EASY RECIPES

These recipes are ideal for small steaks, chops, and cutlets of venison. All of them require slow, moist cooking in a skillet or other container, a method that I consider to be the best—or at least most foolproof—way to handle venison. Some other steak specialties, such as blackened venison or grilled steaks, are discussed in other chapters.

Gulf Coast Spanish Venison

In addition to the French and Cajuns, the Spanish had a great influence on the cooking along the Gulf Coast from Tampa to Mexico. This recipe is of Spanish origin and I adapted it from a little cookbook published by Meme's restaurant at Bon Secour, Alabama, a remote fishing village across the bay from Mobile.

2 pounds good venison steak or chops
2 cups chopped tomatoes
2 large green bell peppers, chopped
2 medium onions, chopped
2 cloves garlic, minced
2 cups hot water
lard or cooking oil
salt and pepper

If the venison is very tough, beat it with a meat mallet or the edge of a plate. Serving-size pieces of steak are easier to use than single rounds of leg. Heat a little lard or cooking oil in a heavy skillet and brown the steaks. (Lard, being hog fat, is frowned upon by modern health experts, but it sure does make a tasty dish. Vegetable oil will also work well and is usually recommended these days. I never measure the lard by volume, and the amount needed will depend partly on the diameter of the skillet. I like it about ⅛ inch deep.) When using a small skillet, you'll have to brown the steak in two or more batches. As soon as each batch browns slightly on both sides, set it aside to drain on several layers of paper toweling, or, better, on a brown grocery bag. After browning all the pieces of steak, sauté the onion, garlic, and peppers until the onions are transparent. Add the chopped tomatoes. It's best to have fresh tomatoes that have ripened on the vine. If these aren't available, use a 16-ounce can of whole tomatoes, chopped. Next, put the steak into the skillet and add the water. (If you have canned tomatoes, use all the juice from the can and add enough water to make 2 cups of liquid.) Add salt and pepper to taste. Bring the mixture to a boil, reduce the heat, cover tightly, and simmer for an hour.

Move the venison about from time to time, making sure that the bottom pieces don't burn. Also taste for seasoning, adding a little salt and pepper if needed. I like quite a bit of black pepper on mine, but suit yourself. Serve with rice, bread, and a green salad. I always allow at least ½ pound of meat per person. This recipe is easy to adjust; for each pound of steak, merely add one more chopped onion, one chopped clove of garlic, one chopped green pepper, one chopped tomato, and 1 cup of water. If you're cooking quite a bit of meat, it's best to simmer this dish in a stove-top Dutch oven instead of in a skillet.

Loin Cutlets with Watercress

Watercress grows wild in suitable cool-water streams over much of the United States and is available to most outdoorsmen. This unusual recipe was adapted from *Gourmet Cooking for Free* by Bradford Angier. He calls the meat "back steaks," which means that they are cut from the long strip of meat that runs atop either side of the backbone. These pieces require no tenderizing, especially if they are cut thick and served rare. Angier didn't say whether the steaks are cooked with the aid of oil or grease, so I assume he uses the dry-skillet method. I like to use a cast-iron skillet, sprinkled with a little salt, which helps season the sauce.

> 2 pounds loin cutlets, cut 2 inches thick
> salt and pepper
> 1 medium onion, finely chopped
> ½ cup watercress, chopped
> ½ teaspoon powdered mustard seeds
> 1 cup dry sherry

In a small saucepan, mix and heat the sherry, onion, watercress, and mustard. Keep warm. Heat a cast-iron skillet and cook the cutlets over high heat for 2 minutes on one side. Turn and cook for 2 minutes on the other side. Turn the cutlets again and slowly pour in the wine sauce. Cook on high heat for several minutes. (Angier says 2 minutes, but I prefer 4 or 5. In any case, the steaks should be served rare or medium rare.) Serve the steaks on heated plates and pour the watercress sauce over them. The meat should be eaten immediately; Angier says that hot peas and boiled potatoes "will make an adventure of this."

Venison Cutlets with Currant Sauce

Red currant jelly is frequently used in game cookery, and this recipe uses it in a pan sauce. It's easy and good.

> 2 pounds thin venison cutlets
> ½ cup cooking oil
> red wine vinegar
> flour
> ¼ cup red currant jelly
> salt and pepper

I like to make this dish from the loin, merely slicing off ¼-inch pieces. If similar cuts are made from leg meat, use a commercial meat tenderizer, following the directions on the box, or pound the pieces with a meat mallet. Put the cutlets in a glass container and sprinkle them with red wine vinegar. Marinate at room temperature for an hour or so. When you are ready to cook, salt and pepper the cutlets on both sides. Put a cup or so of flour into a bag, add the cutlets, and shake. Do not pat the cutlets dry before shaking them in the flour; the idea is to get a rather thick coating on the meat, so that some of it will come off in the pan and contribute to the gravy.

Heat the oil. Fry the steaks for 2 or 3 minutes, turning once. Do not overcook. Medium rare is best. Take up the steaks and put them onto a heated serving platter. Using a wooden spoon, quickly scrape up any flour that has stuck to the bottom of the pan. Stir with the wooden spoon in one hand and sprinkle in a little flour with the other hand. Stir in a little water and the red currant jelly. Simmer and stir until the gravy is as thick as you like it. Add a little salt and pepper if needed. Pour the gravy over the cutlets and serve.

Venison Steaks with Wine Sauce

Here's a recipe that is bound to be a hit if you've got tender venison to start with. Use loin or tenderloin cuts, or tenderize leg steaks. Cut the steaks ½ inch thick.

2 pounds tender venison steaks
½ cup butter
½ cup dry red wine
½ cup sliced mushrooms
¼ cup fresh parsley, minced
1 tablespoon onion, minced
2 tablespoons red currant or tart plum jelly
salt and pepper to taste

Melt the butter in a skillet and fry the steaks for 3 minutes on each side. Drain the steaks on a heated platter and sprinkle with salt and freshly ground black pepper. Sauté the mushrooms and onions for a few minutes. Add the wine, parsley, and jelly. Heat for a few minutes, then pour the sauce over the steaks. Serve hot.

Easy Venison Chops

This recipe can be cooked with venison rib chops, or with steaks or cutlets from the loin or tenderloin. If round steaks or cutlets from the leg muscles are used, tenderize them first. The measures call for 2 pounds, which should feed four hungry people. If you are using bone-in chops, consider adding a few more. I usually prepare this dish in a large skillet, but it can also be made in a Dutch oven, provided that the meat is browned in batches.

2 pounds venison chops or cutlets
1 can mushroom soup (10¾-ounce size)
1 soup can of water
cooking oil
flour
salt and pepper to taste

7

Salt and pepper the chops, then shake them in a sack of flour. Heat a little cooking oil in a large skillet or stove-top Dutch oven and brown the chops on both sides. (Brown in two or more batches if necessary.) Mix the soup and a can of water, then pour the liquid into the skillet or Dutch oven. Bring to a boil, reduce the heat, cover tightly, and simmer for an hour, or until the meat is fork tender. Turn the chops after about 30 minutes so that the bottom pieces are rotated, and add a little salt and pepper to the gravy. The gravy should be served over rice or mashed potatoes, along with green beans, hot bread, and a colorful salad.

This makes a good camp dish because the ingredients are easy to pack in and handle without breaking the jar or spilling the box.

Cutlets and Yogurt

I usually prepare this dish when my good wife goes on her yogurt diet and we've got a ready supply of the stuff in the refrigerator. Sometimes I use a marinade, also made with yogurt, and sometimes I don't, depending on the cut of meat. When using tenderloin, cut it into 2-inch wheels, then butterfly it, giving a "cutlet" about an inch thick, and skip the marinade. When making cutlets from a leg muscle, cut them about an inch thick and marinate them for several hours in a mixture of 1 cup of yogurt, juice from one medium onion, and pepper. (This marinade is enough for 2 pounds of venison.) Mix the marinade in a non-metallic container and toss the cutlets in it, coating all sides. Marinate in the refrigerator for several hours. When you are ready to cook, proceed with the recipe.

> 2 pounds venison cutlets
> flour
> ¼ to ½ cup cooking oil
> ½ cup yogurt
> 1 tablespoon Worcestershire sauce
> 1 teaspoon celery salt
> ½ teaspoon black pepper
> water

Put the flour into a bag and shake the cutlets in it. If the meat is tough, tenderize it with a meat mallet or by pounding it in a criss-cross manner with the edge of a plate. Heat the oil in a skillet and brown the cutlets. Remove them and stir in 1 cup of water. Return the cutlets to the skillet, fitting them in neatly. Mix the yogurt, Worcestershire sauce, celery salt, and black pepper in a bowl, then pour the mixture over the cutlets. Bring to a high heat but not to a boil. Reduce heat, cover tightly, and simmer for an hour, or until the cutlets are tender. Check from time to time, add a little water if needed, and stir to prevent the bottom from burning. Serve with steamed rice, bread, and vegetables. Spoon the pan gravy over the cutlets and rice.

Dutch Oven Steak

I like to cook this dish all day on very low heat using a cast-iron stove-top Dutch oven with a tight lid. I got the recipe from a booklet called *Wild Game Recipes,* published by the North Carolina Wildlife Resources Commission, to which it was submitted by Mamie Rivenbark.

> 3 pounds venison steaks or cutlets
> cooking oil
> flour
> 1 large onion
> 1 large green pepper
> 2 cans cream of mushroom soup (10¾-ounce size)
> 2 soup cans water
> salt and pepper to taste

Heat 4 tablespoons of cooking oil in the Dutch oven and brown the steaks. Remove them and sauté the onion and green pepper for a few minutes. Add 2 tablespoons of flour and stir while cooking for five minutes or so. Stir in the water and soup, plus a little salt and pepper. Reduce heat, cover tightly, and simmer all day on very low heat. Serve with mashed potatoes and steamed vegetables.

Easy Oven Cutlets

Here's an easy oven dish that is good enough to make deerslayers of your guests.

> 2 pounds venison cutlets (½ inch thick)
> 1 medium onion, sliced
> 1 can cream of mushroom soup (10¾-ounce size)
> ½ cup dry red wine
> salt and pepper

Preheat the oven to 325 degrees. Grease a ceramic or glass casserole dish suitable for serving on the table. Put the cutlets on the bottom. Add the sliced onions. Spread the soup over the top, then add wine, salt, and pepper. Cover tightly with aluminum foil and bake for 2½ hours. Allow ½ pound of meat per person.

If you love garlic, try adding about 16 whole peeled cloves along with the onions.

Venison, Mushrooms, and Red Wine

I like this recipe prepared with thinly sliced loin, but cutlets from the leg muscle segments also work nicely. If the meat is tough, pound it first with a meat mallet or the edge of a plate.

> 2 pounds venison cutlets, ½ inch thick
> 2 pounds fresh mushrooms
> ½ cup olive oil
> 1 can tomato paste (6-ounce size)
> flour
> 2 cloves garlic, minced
> 1 cup dry red wine
> salt and pepper to taste

Heat the olive oil in a large skillet (or Dutch oven). Salt and pepper the cutlets and dredge in flour. Brown the meat, then drain it on a brown grocery bag. Sauté the mushrooms and garlic for a few minutes. Put the meat back into the skillet. Mix the wine and tomato paste, then stir the mixture into the meat and mushrooms. Cover tightly and simmer for 30 minutes, stirring and turning from time to time. Feeds four to six. Serve along with French-cut beans, mashed potatoes, and other vegetables. I like this with frozen mixed vegetables, especially the San Francisco and California blends.

Cutlets with Anjou Pears

I found this basic recipe in a little book called *Game Cookery,* written by E. N. and Edith Sturdivant in 1967.

> venison cutlets for two
> 1 Anjou pear
> thin slices of onion
> thin slices of lemon
> 1 tablespoon cooking oil
> ¾ cup dark brown sugar
> ¾ cup water
> ¼ cup soy sauce
> ½ teaspoon grated ginger
> salt and pepper to taste

Allow at least ½ pound of venison per person. Loin (or butter-flied tenderloin) works well, and should be about an inch thick. Peel the pear, cut it in half lengthwise, and core it. Salt and pepper the venison. Heat the oil and brown the venison lightly. Place a slice of lemon and a slice of onion atop each piece of meat. Fit the pear halves into the skillet on either side of the meat. Combine all the other ingredients and pour the mixture over the venison and pears. Cover tightly and simmer for 15 minutes. Turn the pears and simmer for another 15 minutes, basting the meat with pan juices from time to time. Serve with rice, green salad, and bread. The Sturdivants recommend peach cobbler with cream for dessert.

TRADITIONAL AND CLASSIC STEAK RECIPES

Many of our old recipes for meat came from game cookery, and such techniques as grilling kabobs have been practiced for thousands of years. Others were developed after domesticated animals became common. In any case, the suggestions below are old favorites from Europe and North America.

Venison Steak Diane

This romantic dish is usually prepared one serving at a time. It can be made at the table with an electric skillet, or on the patio with one of the new burners that fit onto the side of gas grills. When making it with venison, I like to use butterflied loin or tenderloin steaks if I've got them, allowing about ½ pound per person. In any case, the steaks should be tender.

> venison steaks, boneless, for one
> 2 tablespoons butter
> 2 tablespoons dry sherry
> 1 tablespoon brandy
> 1 tablespoon chopped shallots (or small onions)
> 1 teaspoon chopped chives
> salt and pepper to taste

Cut the steak exactly ½-inch thick and then pound it down with a meat mallet until it is ¼-inch thick. While pounding, turn the steak from time to time and sprinkle with salt and pepper. It's best to use freshly ground pepper. Heat the skillet and melt the butter. Cook the steak for about 2 minutes. Turn and cook the other side. Pour a tablespoon of brandy over the steak and set it afire with a match. When it burns out, remove the steak to a warm serving plate. Add the shallots and chives to the pan and stir. Add the sherry and simmer for 2 or 3 minutes, stirring continuously. Pour the pan juices over the steak. Serve immediately.

Venison Stroganoff

Named for a nineteenth-century Russian count, this wonderful dish, usually made with tenderloin of beef, is characterized by fork-tender meat, mushrooms, sour cream, and noodles. (Home-made green noodles, containing spinach, are best, but store-bought egg noodles are satisfactory.) Careful chefs will cut the tenderloin about ¼-inch thick and then pound it down with the smooth side of a meat mallet until it is about ⅛-inch thick. The pounding tenderizes the meat, but tenderloin of venison for the recipe below can be partly frozen and sliced thinly. If you don't have tenderloin, loin or any other good cut of venison can be used. If your meat is at all tough, slice it thinly and use commercial tenderizer on it before proceeding.

> 2 pounds venison tenderloin or loin
> 1 pound sliced mushrooms
> ¼ cup grated onion
> 1¼ cups sour cream
> ½ cup white wine (red or rosé also will do)
> ¼ cup butter (used in two batches)
> ⅛ teaspoon grated nutmeg
> salt and pepper to taste
> egg noodles (cooked separately)

Melt half of the butter in a skillet and sauté the onion for a few minutes, stirring with a wooden spoon. Add the venison slices and sauté for 3 or 4 minutes, stirring constantly. Remove the venison but keep it warm. Quickly melt the rest of the butter and sauté the mushrooms for 5 minutes. Return the meat to the skillet and stir. Add salt, pepper, and nutmeg. Stir in the wine, then the sour cream. Leave the skillet on the heat for another 5 minutes, but do not allow it to boil, lest you have a curdled mess on your hands. Serve over a bed of noodles.

Note: There are hundreds and probably thousands of recipes for stroganoff. The one above is what I consider to be classic.

Others are also good, and I confess I have made it with good venison and a store-bought Hamburger Helper stroganoff package.

Swiss Steak

I must have seen a hundred recipes for this dish. Frankly, I don't know exactly what "Swiss steak" is, since the ingredients vary so much, but the recipes all call for simmering a tough cut for a long while. In any case, one of the best of these recipes for venison came my way from Missouri, not Switzerland.

> 2 pounds thick venison steaks
> 2 large onions, chopped
> 2 large tomatoes, chopped
> 1 rib celery (with green tops), chopped
> ¼ cup Worcestershire sauce
> cooking oil
> flour
> salt and pepper
> mashed potatoes (cooked separately)

Cut the steaks about 1½ inches thick, salt and pepper each side, coat with flour, and pound one side with a meat mallet or the edge of a plate. Coat again with flour and pound the other side. Heat about ¼ cup of oil in a skillet. (The skillet should have a lid.) Quickly brown the steaks on both sides. Add the onion, tomatoes, celery, and Worcestershire sauce. (No water is required.) Reduce heat, cover, and simmer for an hour and a half, or until the meat is fork tender. When you are almost ready to eat, remove the steak from the skillet and put it onto a heated serving platter. Stir the contents of the skillet with a wooden spoon, scraping the bottom, and stir in a little water. Heat and stir until the gravy is as thick as you want it. Spoon a little gravy over the steaks and put the rest into a bowl for serving over mashed potatoes. Also serve with fresh baby lima beans, butter beans, or French-cut green beans.

TWO

Venison Stew Meat

I have known hunters who grind up a whole deer or even an elk into hamburger meat or sausage. Following one formula or another, they add beef suet or pork fat. The results are often tasty, but this method adds fat and cholesterol to one of nature's most healthy red meats.

I suggest a different approach. Instead of grinding the meat, try cutting it into cubes like supermarket stew meat. Such meat can also be easily wrapped and frozen in small packages, and it is easy to cook. Cutting the meat into chunks doesn't require special equipment or a degree in butchering. Remember that stew meat can be ground into hamburger before it is cooked, making it even more versatile.

Stew meat is best wrapped tightly in white paper and properly marked. Units of 1 pound work better for me simply because I most often use 1- or 2-pound units in recipes, not the odd-sized packages of stew meat found in our American supermarkets. Of course, the home butcher can also trim all the fat and connective tissue from the venison before freezing it. If ½ pound of meat is needed, score and break a package in half. The remainder can be wrapped again and returned to the freezer.

EASY STEW MEAT RECIPES

These recipes set forth some easy ways to cook stew meat. Some of them call for frozen vegetable mixes for soup, gumbo, and stew. Available in supermarkets, these mixes save time and money because you buy only enough of any one major ingredient to cook the dish at hand. (In other words, you don't have to buy a whole bunch of celery in order to get one or two stalks.) Of course, garden-fresh vegetables are better, so use them if they are available. Remember also that dried or canned vegetable mixes can be used and come in handy for cooking in camp.

Easy Venison Stew

> 2 pounds cubed venison meat
> milk (for marinade)
> 1 tablespoon vegetable oil
> 1 package frozen stew vegetables (16-ounce size)
> 1 can tomatoes (16-ounce size)
> 1 medium onion, diced
> ½ tablespoon parsley
> 1 teaspoon salt
> ½ teaspoon pepper

Put the venison into a glass container and cover it with milk. Marinate for 12 hours, or overnight. When you are ready to cook, heat 1 tablespoon of oil in a stove-top Dutch oven or soup pot. Lightly brown the venison and the diced onion. Add enough water to almost cover the meat, bring to a boil, reduce the heat, cover tightly, and simmer for about 2 hours, or until the meat is tender. Chop the canned tomatoes and add them to the pot, along with the juice from the can. Add the vegetable mix, parsley, salt, and pepper. Bring to a boil, reduce the heat, cover, and simmer for 30 minutes, or until the vegetables are tender.

Note: Remember that you can add reasonable amounts of other vegetables if you've got them on hand, such as mushrooms.

Easy Venison Soup

Compared to the stew above, this soup recipe calls for diced vegetables and diced meat. When you thaw the venison, trim it and cut it into ½-inch cubes.

1 pound diced venison
milk (for marinade)
1 package frozen soup vegetable mix (16-ounce size)
1 can tomatoes (16-ounce size)
6 green onions
½ teaspoon salt
¼ to ½ teaspoon pepper
2 cups water or stock

Using a glass container, soak the venison in milk for 12 hours or overnight. When you are ready to cook, drain the meat and put it into a suitable pot with water or venison, chicken, or beef stock. Chop the tomatoes and put them, along with the juice from the can, into the pot. Bring to a boil, cover, reduce heat, and simmer for an hour and a half. (If your venison is very tender, you can cut the cooking time.) Chop the onions, including about half of the green tops, and put them into the pot, along with the soup mix vegetables, salt, and pepper. Personally, I prefer more black pepper, especially if it is freshly ground. But don't overdo it. Make a rather bland soup for your guests, then have a pepper mill on the table for use in individual servings. Eat this soup with hot French bread.

A.D.'s Smother-Fried Venison Cubes

Thaw your cubed venison, then pound it or sprinkle on some meat tenderizer (following directions on the package), or both, depending on how tough it is. Salt and pepper the meat to taste and shake it in a bag of flour. Heat ½ inch of peanut oil in a large skillet and brown the meat. Drain it on a brown grocery bag. Pour off most of the oil. Add a little flour and heat it in the remaining oil and pan dredgings, as when making a roux. Stir for a few minutes until the flour starts to brown. Gradually pour in some hot water, stirring constantly, until you have a thin gravy. Add the meat to the gravy, sprinkle on a little salt and pepper, cover tightly, reduce the heat, and simmer. Stir in a little more water from time to time, if needed. Make a large batch of sourdough biscuits while the meat simmers. How long? For 2 whole hours, if you can stand the aroma for that long. This stuff is good. Of course, you serve the gravy over the biscuit halves. In camp, it is permissible to sop the gravy with the biscuits.

Easy Venison Gumbo

A gumbo can be simple or complex. Some people make a ritual of it, starting with a roux. A gumbo recipe can have a mile-long list of ingredients or a relatively short one, but it really ought to have some okra in it, which gives a gumbo its distinctive texture. Here's an easy recipe for venison:

> 2 pounds cubed venison
> ½ pound venison or beef sausage in casing
> baking soda marinade (optional)
> 1 package frozen gumbo vegetables (16-ounce size)
> 1 can tomatoes (16-ounce size)
> 2 cups venison stock or beef bouillon
> 3 cloves garlic, minced
> salt
> pepper
> rice (cooked separately)

For soda marinade, mix 1 tablespoon baking soda into 1 quart of water. Put cubed venison into a glass container and pour the marinade over it. Refrigerate overnight or for 8 hours. Drain venison and rinse in cold water. Put the frozen vegetables out to thaw. In a small stove-top Dutch oven or pot, heat the stock and add tomatoes along with the juice from the can. Add the venison, cover tightly, and simmer for 2 hours or until the venison is tender. Add the vegetable mix, garlic, salt, and pepper. Slice the sausage into wheels and add to the gumbo. Cover and simmer for 30 minutes. Serve in bowls with cooked rice.

To cook the rice, put 2 cups of water into a pot or boiler of suitable size and add a little butter. Bring to a boil, add 1 cup of regular long-grain rice, and return to a very light boil. Immediately reduce the heat, cover tightly, and simmer for 20 minutes. Don't peek. Remove the rice from the stove and place the bottom of the pan into a larger container of cold water. If you've done this right, the rice won't be mushy.

Note: The gumbo vegetable mix in this recipe is not a vegetable soup or stew mix. It will have "gumbo" on it in large letters. If you use another mix or mix your own, remember that this recipe should have at least 1 cup of cut okra in it.

Easy Venison Ragout

A ragout can be plain or fancy, but it is basically meat that is seared (without flour or batter) and then simmered for a long time in a stock. Here's a very easy recipe:

> 2 pounds venison chunks
> 1 cup milk
> 1 can beef broth (10½-ounce size)
> 1 cup chopped pecans
> 1 cup red wine
> cooking oil
> salt and pepper

Cut the meat into 1-inch cubes, put it into a glass container, pour the milk over it, and refrigerate for 8 hours or longer, stirring a time or two. When you are ready to cook, heat a little oil in a large skillet or Dutch oven. Drain the meat and brown it lightly in the hot oil. Pour off the excess. Salt and pepper the meat. Add the broth and bring to a bubble. Reduce the heat, cover tightly, and simmer for an hour and a half. Stir from time to time. Add the wine and pecans. Simmer for another 30 minutes. Serve over rice or mashed potatoes.

Note: The last time I cooked this recipe, I used a cup of mild new-crop acorns. I first heated them in the oven until they popped open, then hulled them and added them to the ragout. They were sweet acorns, however, and I must point out most acorns will be too bitter for using in this manner.

Easy Camp Stew

This stew is easy to make and calls mostly for canned ingredients (which are easy to store) plus venison, which can be kept in an ice chest. A pack of frozen venison, wrapped in several newspapers, will keep a long time in a foam chest. Wrap the packaged venison in the papers and then put the whole thing back into the freezer for several hours, thereby getting even the papers ice cold. Fresh meat can also be used, but generally venison should be aged for at least a week before cooking; if fresh meat is used, try the tenderloin or loin instead of tougher meat. In any case, I normally cook this recipe in a stove-top Dutch oven, but a large skillet will also work.

>2 pounds cubed venison
>2 tablespoons oil or butter
>1 large onion, chopped
>1 green bell pepper, chopped
>1 can whole-kernel corn (16-ounce size)
>1 can whole tomatoes (16-ounce size)
>1 can kidney beans (16-ounce size)
>1 tablespoon chili powder
>1 teaspoon salt

Heat the oil and brown the meat slightly, along with the chopped pepper and onion. Open the cans of vegetables and drain the liquid from the cans into the pot. Cook and stir until the liquid is reduced by half. Then add the corn, tomatoes, beans, chili powder, and salt. Stir until everything is hot, then serve in bowls. This dish goes with any kind of bread, including crackers, and feeds four to six people.

CLASSIC AND TRADITIONAL STEW MEAT RECIPES

Since venison profits from long simmering, many classic stews and recipes can be made with it and were probably developed, ages ago, with venison or aurochs, the extinct wild European forerunner of cattle. In any case, these dishes are ideal for introducing people to venison, since many of the recipes have familiar flavors and names.

Irish Stew with Venison

According to a friend of mine, the Irish invented everything from gunpowder to spinning reels. When I point out the Irish potato (which is what many Americans call an ordinary Idaho potato) was originally grown in America, he doesn't want to hear it—but he'll eat this stew, which is made with American white-tailed deer instead of an old Irish sheep. This is a good recipe for cooking in camp because it doesn't require lots of dainty or fragile ingredients.

> 3 pounds venison stew meat
> milk for marinade (optional)
> 2 pounds potatoes (preferably small)
> 1 pound onions (preferably small)
> 1½ cups water or venison stock
> ½ tablespoon parsley
> 1 teaspoon thyme
> 1 teaspoon salt
> ½ teaspoon pepper

If the meat is tough or strong, marinate it overnight in milk. Drain the meat and trim it. Put the meat into a suitable pan and add the water or stock. Bring to boil, reduce heat, cover, and simmer for 2 hours or until the meat is tender. (If you have very tender venison, the previous step can be omitted.)

Preheat the oven to 325 degrees. Peel the potatoes and onions. Slice a potato thinly and line the bottom of a Dutch oven with it. Cover the potatoes with sliced onion. Then add the meat from the pan, but retain the liquid. Next, add the rest of the onions, either whole or quartered, depending on size. Sprinkle on the parsley, thyme, salt, and pepper. Add the rest of the potatoes, whole or quartered, again depending on size. Measure the liquid from the pan and add enough water to make 1½ cups. Pour the liquid over the stew. Cover tightly and bake for 2 hours.

Venison Hungarian Goulash

Here's an old recipe that was no doubt originally made with venison or other game. In my version, I use a lot of mild Hungarian paprika, which gives good color as well as a pleasing flavor.

> 3 pounds cubed venison
> milk for marinade (optional)
> 5 fresh tomatoes, peeled and chopped
> 1 large onion, peeled and diced
> 1 bell pepper, diced
> 3 cloves garlic, minced
> 1 cup venison stock or beef broth
> 1 cup red wine
> 5 tablespoons mild Hungarian paprika
> 1 teaspoon salt
> ½ teaspoon black pepper
> egg noodles (cooked separately)

Trim the meat, put it into a glass or ceramic container, cover with milk, and refrigerate overnight. Rinse the meat and let it drain. In a large skillet or Dutch oven, lightly brown the meat, chopped onion, and minced garlic. Add the venison stock, bring to boil, reduce heat, cover tightly, and simmer on very low heat for 2 hours. (If the lid lets steam escape, you may need to add a little water.) Add the tomatoes, bell pepper, paprika, salt, and black pepper. Simmer for 1 hour. Add the wine, adjust seasoning if needed, and simmer for another 30 minutes. Serve over hot noodles sprinkled with mild paprika.

J. P. Betsill's Georgia Brunswick Stew

There has been a lot of discussion about where Brunswick stew came from and what the original contained. Brunswick, Georgia,

22

is a good candidate, and the original was probably made with game. Some authorities specify rabbit and squirrel. But what about venison? In any case, the following recipe is very good, and I adapted it from a booklet called *Wild Game Recipes*, published some time ago by the North Carolina Wildlife Resources Commission. This recipe makes a large batch and is ideal for feeding 25 or 30 people. Before proceeding, however, make sure that your pot is large enough to hold it. The recipe also calls for grinding all the meat. If you don't have a sausage mill, try chopping it finely with a chef's knife. A food processor will work, but remember that you don't want mush.

> 4 pounds venison
> 4 pounds rabbit
> 4 pounds pork
> 1 gallon white shoe-peg corn
> 1 gallon canned tomatoes
> 1½ pounds onions
> 3 large bell peppers
> 4 tablespoons soy sauce
> ¼ cup Worcestershire sauce
> salt and black pepper to taste

Trim the fat from the venison. You can also trim the fat from the pork if you are on a diet or have cholesterol problems. (The original Betsill recipe calls for Boston butt, which usually weighs about 4 pounds, but I have used leaner cuts of pork to advantage.) For flavor, it's best to leave some part of the fat on the pork. Boil all the meat until tender, and then grind it. Cook the peppers and onions until tender, then grind them too. (It's best to boil the meat long before you are ready to cook. Chilled meat is easier to grind than warm meat. Also, I like to add a few bay leaves to the pot in which the meat is boiled. Remember to save part of the broth, which may be needed to thin the stew.)

Mix everything in a large pot. When it starts to bubble, reduce the heat, cover tightly, and simmer for an hour. Stir from to time to time, tasting and adding a little salt or pepper if needed. Also, add a little broth as needed to thin the stew to your liking. If the stew is to be served in bowls, you'll want it on the thin side. If it is to be served on a plate along with barbecue, you'll want it thicker so that it won't run all over the plate.

Venison Sauce Piquante

The Cajuns put so much stuff into a recipe (and keep adding to the list in an effort to outdo one another) that it's hard to tell what's absolute and what's not. But they cook up some good stuff, and I have tried to keep the recipe below to a reasonable length. It is best prepared in a 13-inch cast-iron skillet.

> 2 pounds venison, cut into 1-inch cubes
> ¼ pound smoked bacon
> 4 medium onions, diced
> ½ cup green onion tops or parsley, chopped
> 1 bell pepper, diced
> 1 stalk celery with green tops, sliced
> 2 large red tomatoes, chopped
> 8 ounces mushrooms, sliced
> 2 cloves garlic, minced
> juice of 1 lemon
> 1 can tomato paste (6-ounce size)
> water
> flour
> 1 teaspoon salt
> ½ teaspoon red pepper flakes or hot sauce
> rice (cooked separately)

Fry the bacon in a large skillet until crisp. (If you don't have a wide skillet, a stove-top Dutch oven will do.) Remove the bacon and drain. Brown the venison in the bacon drippings, remove with a slotted spoon, and drain. Put 2 tablespoons of flour into the skillet, mix into the bacon drippings, and stir on low heat until you have a brown roux. Stir in the tomato paste, lemon juice, and 2 cups of water. Add the onions, green tops, garlic, celery, bell pepper, tomatoes, and mushrooms. Cover and simmer 30

24

minutes. Crumble the bacon and add it to the skillet, along with the browned venison. Add 2 cups of water, salt, and pepper. Bring to a boil, reduce heat, cover, and simmer for 4 hours. Stir from time to time, adding a little water if needed, and adjust seasonings as you go. Serve in bowls over rice.

Venison Bourguignonne

This wonderful stew is usually made these days with lean red meat, red wine, and mushrooms; it works nicely with venison. This is one of my favorites.

> 2 pounds venison
> ½ pound salt pork
> 8 ounces fresh mushrooms, sliced
> 10 shallots or small pearl onions
> lots of red wine and a little water
> salt and freshly ground pepper
> 1 teaspoon fresh thyme or ½ teaspoon dried
> 2 bay leaves
> flour
> butter
> parsley (for garnish)

Cut the venison into 1-inch cubes. Place these into a non-metallic container and cover with red wine. Marinate for several hours or overnight in the refrigerator. When you are ready to cook, dice the salt pork into ½-inch cubes or smaller and fry in a skillet until you have nicely browned pieces (cracklings) and a good amount of fat. Remove the cracklings with a slotted spoon and drain on a brown bag. Peel and brown the shallots. (I leave them whole.) Remove and drain them beside the salt pork.

Drain the venison and retain the marinade. Shake the cubes in a bag with a little flour and brown in the skillet. Add the thyme and bay leaves. Mix the leftover marinade with a little water (about 3 parts wine and 1 part water) and pour the mixture over the meat. Then pour in more wine and water until the meat is barely covered. Bring to a light boil, reduce heat, cover tightly, and simmer for an hour. Add the cracklings, shallots, freshly ground black pepper, and salt. Cover and simmer for an hour, stirring and adjusting the seasoning from time to time. During the last hour, sauté the mushrooms in butter and add them to the stew. Garnish with sprigs of fresh parsley and serve.

Some people flame this stew with brandy shortly before serving, but if I've got good brandy, I prefer to hold it for sipping with coffee after the meal.

Bigos

This old Polish dish was at one time traditionally eaten after the hunt and was made with bear and other game. This recipe calls for venison and bear. If you don't have the bear, substitute lean pork.

> ½ pound venison, cut into cubes
> ½ pound bear meat, cut into cubes
> ½ pound venison sausage, in ½-inch wheels
> ½ pound bacon, cut into pieces
> 2 cans sauerkraut (16-ounce size)
> 1 can beef broth (10½-ounce size)
> 1 large onion, diced
> 8 ounces fresh mushrooms, sliced
> 1 cup wine
> 1 tablespoon mild paprika
> salt and pepper

In a stove-top Dutch oven, fry the bacon until crisp. Remove it with a slotted spoon and drain. Sauté the onion and mushrooms in the drippings for a few minutes, then remove and drain them. Pour off all but about ¼ cup of the drippings. Brown the venison, bear (or lean pork), and sausage. Add the bacon, onions, mushrooms, broth, wine, paprika, salt, and pepper. Stir and bring to a light boil. Cover, reduce heat, and simmer for 2 hours. Shortly before you are ready to eat, drain the sauerkraut and stir it into the dish. Serve hot.

Venison Ardennes

Americans don't eat much boiled meat, except in stews and soups, and that is a pity. Venison is especially good when boiled, and in the past has been popular in England, France, and other parts of Europe. According to George Leonard Herter, co-author of *Bull Cook and Authentic Historical Recipes and Practices,* this recipe originated in the Ardennes forest of Belgium, where plenty of deer roam. I've also seen Ardennes recipes from France.

> 2 pounds venison
> salt and pepper
> cold water
> 1 cup apple cider vinegar
> ¼ cup flour
> 1 medium onion, chopped
> ¼ teaspoon ground cloves
> ½ teaspoon ground ginger
> ½ teaspoon salt
> ⅛ teaspoon black pepper

Trim the meat carefully and cut it into bite-size pieces. Place the meat into a pot, cover it with water, and add salt and pepper to taste. Bring the liquid to a boil, reduce heat, cover, and simmer for an hour, or until the pieces are very tender. While the venison simmers, mix the flour and enough cold water to form a thin paste. In a saucepan, mix the paste, vinegar, onion, cloves, ginger, salt, and black pepper. (I usually use black pepper, as Herter directed, but purists may choose to use white pepper in a white sauce.) Heat the mixture, stirring constantly, until you have a smooth gravy.

Drain the venison quickly and serve the gravy over it. Both should be hot, so make the sauce when the venison is almost ready.

Chili con Carne

This great American classic recipe for stew meat came to us from the Indians of the Southwest. The term *chili con carne* means, simply, "hot peppers with meat," and those ingredients, along with a little water, are all you need to cook it. In fact, some purists insist that no beans be allowed in the pot, although they might eat separately cooked beans with the dish. I'll leave it up to you, but I do want to point out that venison stew meat is ideal for cooking chili since it can be simmered for a long time without coming apart.

> 4 pounds venison stew meat
> 5 strips bacon
> 1 medium onion, diced
> 4 cloves garlic, minced
> 2 tablespoons prepared chili powder
> 1 tablespoon cumin seeds, crushed
> 1 tablespoon salt
> water

In a stove-top Dutch oven, cook the bacon until crisp, and drain it. In the bacon drippings, brown the meat, onion, and garlic. Cover the meat with water, and add the chili powder, cumin seeds, and salt. Bring to a boil, reduce heat, cover tightly, and simmer for several hours—the longer the better, within reason. I have cooked it all day. Stir it from time to time, and add a little more water if needed.

Serve the chili in bowls along with crackers and pinto beans. If you insist, add a can or two of pinto beans to the pot during the last few minutes of cooking. This recipe is also good with a little rice (cooked separately) mixed into the bowl.

In most American homes these days chili is cooked with ground meat. Of course, ground venison is ideal for chili, and I include an easy recipe for it in the next chapter.

Arawak Pepperpot

This dish, popular in parts of the southern Caribbean and Guyana, is made with several meats these days, but all versions are flavored by cassareep, a condiment made from the roots of cassava plants.

It can be purchased in some Caribbean markets, and by mail order. Although pepperpot is now made mostly with beef, pork, and sometimes chicken, it was originally cooked with such meat as agouti, iguana, and guinea pig, and maybe duck and turtle. This recipe is my own, calling for venison and other meats, but no chicken. If you've got an armadillo or an agouti—true Arawak fare—substitute a pound of it for the pork.

> 2 pounds venison
> 1 pound lean pork
> 1 pound oxtail
> 2 pigs feet, split in half
> ½ cup cassareep
> 2 or more hot chili peppers
> salt

Put all of the ingredients except the peppers into a Dutch oven or a suitable pot and cover with water. Tie the peppers in a piece of cloth or gauze and drop them into the pot. Bring to a boil and simmer for at least 2 hours, or until the meat is tender. Add a little more water if needed, but remember that the sauce should be quite thick. It's best to simmer on very low heat and stir from time to time. When the stew is ready, remove the peppers before serving. Pepperpot should be eaten with rice.

Remember this dish can be cooked in a pot suspended over a campfire.

THREE

Ground Venison

In recent years, more and more hunters have mixed beef suet or pork fat into their ground venison, or have permitted commercial meat processors to do so. The proportions vary from one practitioner to another, depending, perhaps, on how much beef suet or scrap pork needs to be used up. Some authorities say to mix it half and half. Others go three parts venison to two parts beef suet or fatty pork, and others recommend three to one. From a culinary viewpoint, I support this practice, especially for ground meat that is going to be grilled, broiled, or browned in a skillet. Since venison is very lean, the fat helps both taste and texture. The taste factor comes about, I think, partly because the chunks of beef suet or fatty pork tend to "try" out. That is, the grease tends to cook out, leaving a tasty tidbit somewhat similar to cracklings. This is especially true of patties that are grilled or broiled.

While the resulting ground meat and fat combination may be quite toothsome, modern health authorities have warned that animal fat is not good for humans. A doctor in Florida wrote me a long letter concerning this matter, saying that beef suet is poison. He said that he mixes canola or peanut oil into the venison. I would also like to point out here that there is no great advantage to adding any kind of oil or fat to ground meat that is to be used in recipes for spaghetti sauce and similar dishes.

For versatility and other reasons, I think that it's best by far to grind the meat shortly before it is cooked. Then you can add the fat if it is needed—or leave it out if it isn't needed. This is best accomplished by packaging all the venison as stew meat instead of having it ground as hamburger. Then it can be ground as needed at home. It's best to grind the meat when it is very cold or partly frozen. I recommend that the stew meat be put into 1-pound packages. Then use as many packages as you need, adding pork or beef if desired. Larger cuts of venison, even whole hams, can be reduced to cubes and then ground into burger as needed.

There are several grinders on the market, including electric models. For home use, a hand-cranked unit is fine. I use one that clamps onto a table top. Other grinders are discussed in the sausage section of chapter 11. Meat can also be "ground" in a food processor, but the results are not always satisfactory.

I believe that freshly ground meat is always better than meat that has been ground and then frozen. Meat keeps better in chunks. The same is true of ground beef from a supermarket. I highly recommend that anyone interested in good hamburger should invest in a grinder and buy chunks of meat that can be cubed and ground. The result is better and often cheaper. (I've seen 20-pound chunks of sirloin tip for sale cheaper per pound than small packages of ordinary fatty ground beef.) Of course, such large pieces of meat can be trimmed of fat and tissue before being ground, or you can add beef suet, if you want some fat. You can also add pork or lamb to beef or venison, making your own mix. I, for one, love lean pork ground in with venison or beef—or with beaver, for that matter.

I'm not offering a series of formulas for mixing ground venison and fat because I want to encourage the reader to use no fat at all if the recipe doesn't require it. True, there will be a little difference in texture, which is acceptable in most recipes. For burgers to be grilled or fried, ground meat without fat needs a binder, such as egg. I sometimes save fat trimmed from beef to grind along with the venison, or I use fatty pork, such as picnic hams (cut the meat and fat into chunks, then mix it with the venison chunks before grinding).

All in all, I have learned that ground venison works surprisingly well without much fat, and I wonder whether the nation's hunters, and writers of cookbooks, might have been sold a bill of fat by the nation's meat cutters. In any case, here are some of my favorite recipes for ground venison.

Venison Spaghetti

In my opinion, spaghetti is improved by sauce that has simmered for several hours. Ground venison holds up well under simmering, and I think it beats beef for cooking spaghetti sauce. I give no instructions for cooking the spaghetti, as it is usually best to follow the directions on the package. (If you make your own pasta, then you're way ahead of me on this count.) In any case, remember that the best sauce in the world won't excuse spaghetti that has stuck together in the pot.

> 2 pounds ground venison
> ½ pound fresh mushrooms
> 2 large onions, chopped
> 2 cloves garlic, minced
> ¼ cup olive oil
> 1 can Italian tomatoes (28-ounce size)
> 1 can tomato paste (6-ounce size)
> 1 tablespoon chili powder
> 1 tablespoon sugar
> ¾ teaspoon Italian seasoning
> 2 bay leaves
> salt and pepper to taste
> good red wine
> thin spaghetti (12-ounce package)
> freshly grated Parmesan cheese (optional)

In a large skillet, sauté the onion and garlic for a few minutes in the olive oil. Add the ground venison. Stir with a wooden spoon until the meat is lightly browned, about 5 minutes on medium-low heat. Stir in the mushrooms. Add the tomatoes and the liquid from the can. Stir in the tomato paste plus half a can of water. Stir in the chili powder, sugar, salt, pepper, Italian seasoning, and whole bay leaves. (An Italian seasoning mix is available in spice jars. If you don't have it on hand, try ¼ teaspoon each of crushed dried thyme, basil, and oregano.) Slowly simmer uncovered for at least 3 hours on very low heat. Stir from time to time, and add a little water if it is needed to prevent the bottom from burning or sticking. (If you can't watch the pot, cover it with a tight-fitting, self-basting lid, which will help keep enough liquid in the sauce.)

About 20 minutes before you are ready to serve, taste the sauce for seasonings, adding a little more if needed. Uncork the wine, take a sip, and pour ½ cup into the sauce. Let the rest of the wine breathe uncorked before serving your guests. Cook the spaghetti according to the directions on the package, grate the cheese, and prepare a huge tossed salad. About 5 minutes before eating, heat a loaf of Italian bread. Get out a red-and-white checkered tablecloth. Light the candle. Pour the wine. Eat, drink, and enjoy.

This recipe will feed four to six people of normal appetite. Actually, however, I prefer lots of sauce on my spaghetti, and this recipe can be stretched a little to serve even eight people by cooking 16 ounces of spaghetti instead of 12. Just have plenty of good bread and salad—and sprinkle on lots of Parmesan cheese.

Spaghetti and Venison Meatballs

I normally cook this with the aid of a large skillet and a small one, or a small skillet and a Dutch oven.

> 2 pounds ground venison
> ¼ cup cooking oil (or olive oil)
> 1 can tomatoes (16-ounce size)
> 1 can tomato paste (6-ounce size)
> 2 large onions
> 2 cloves garlic
> 2 tablespoons fresh parsley
> ½ tablespoon Italian seasoning
> salt and pepper
> Parmesan cheese, grated
> 8 ounces spaghetti (cooked separately)

In the large skillet or Dutch oven, heat the oil and sauté the onions and garlic. Chop the tomatoes and add them to the Dutch oven, along with the juice from the can, tomato paste, parsley, and seasonings. Stir, cover, and simmer for an hour or longer, stirring from time to time.

Shortly before you are ready to eat, cook the spaghetti. Add a little salt and pepper to the ground venison and shape it into balls a little smaller than a golf ball. Heat a little oil in the small skillet and brown a batch of the meatballs. Add these to the main pot of sauce and brown another batch of meatballs, continuing until you have all the meatballs browned and into the pot. Simmer for a few minutes, then serve atop spaghetti. Sprinkle with grated cheese. Have plenty of garlic bread and green salad.

Venison Meatballs

Here's a basic dish that I cook with ground venison, as well as with ground turtle and other lean meats.

> 2 pounds ground venison
> 1 cup long-grain rice
> 1 can condensed cream of celery soup (10½-ounce size)
> 1 soup can of water
> 8 ounces fresh mushrooms, sliced
> 1 medium onion, diced
> salt and pepper
> ½ cup butter or margarine

Preheat the oven to 350 degrees. Mix a little salt and pepper into the venison and shape it into meatballs, about the size of golf balls. Heat the butter in the skillet and sauté the onion and mushrooms for a few minutes. Remove the onions and mushrooms with a slotted spoon and brown the meatballs. Put the meatballs, onions, and mushrooms into a Dutch oven or a large baking dish with a cover. Sprinkle the uncooked rice over the meat. Mix the soup and water, then pour it over the meat and rice. Cover tightly and put into the oven. Bake for 30 minutes. Stir quickly and add more salt and pepper if needed. Cover again and bake for another 10 or 15 minutes. This recipe feeds four or five.

Venison Lasagna

This dish has always been a favorite of my family, and recently we have made it with low-fat yogurt cheese, which is made by putting plain yogurt into a bag made with cheesecloth and suspending it over a bowl for a day or two. The whey drips out and the remainder is a soft cheese, similar in texture to cream cheese. If you don't choose to try yogurt cheese or don't have time to make it, try creamed cottage cheese or ricotta cheese.

1 pound ground venison
2 tablespoons olive oil
1 can tomatoes (18-ounce size)
1 can tomato paste (12-ounce size)
1 medium onion, minced
2 cloves garlic, minced
2 cups yogurt cheese (or substitute)
1 cup Parmesan cheese, grated (used in two batches)
12 ounces shredded mozzarella cheese
8 ounces lasagna noodles, cooked
1 tablespoon parsley
1 teaspoon dried oregano
1 teaspoon dried basil
salt and pepper to taste

In a skillet, sauté the onions, garlic, and venison in hot olive oil. Chop the tomatoes and add them and the juice from the can. Stir in the tomato paste, oregano, basil, parsley, and salt. Bring to a boil, stir, reduce heat, and simmer for 20 minutes. While it simmers, preheat the oven to 350 degrees and cook the noodles according to the directions on the package.

Mix the yogurt cheese and ½ cup of the Parmesan cheese. Remove ½ cup of the meat sauce and set aside. In a large baking dish (13 x 9 x 2 inches) alternate layers of noodles, sauce, mozzarella cheese, and yogurt–Parmesan cheese mixture. Spread the reserved sauce on top and sprinkle evenly with the remaining ½ cup of Parmesan. Bake for 45 minutes. Serve with hot Italian or French bread, green salad, and hearty red wine.

Venison Moussaka

This dish is often associated with Greece, but variations are found throughout the Middle East. It depends on eggplant and meat (usually lamb or beef), and is a great one-dish meal when the meat has to be stretched.

The Filling
1 pound ground venison
2 medium eggplants
cooking oil
1 large onion, chopped
1 large tomato, chopped
2 tablespoons tomato paste
2 tablespoons chopped parsley
½ teaspoon ground allspice or cinnamon
salt and pepper

Peel the eggplants and slice them into ½-inch slices. Put the slices onto brown paper bags or towels, without overlapping. Sprinkle them with salt and set them aside for half an hour or longer. Rinse the slices in cold water and pat dry. Heat a little oil in a skillet and sauté the onion and ground venison for about 5 minutes. Stir in the salt, pepper, allspice, tomato, tomato paste, and parsley. Simmer for 15 minutes. Meanwhile, prepare the sauce, and preheat the oven to 350 degrees.

The Sauce
1½ cups hot milk
2½ tablespoons flour
2½ tablespoons butter
1 chicken egg yolk
nutmeg

Melt the butter in a saucepan or small skillet over low heat. Add the flour and stir slowly until blended. Heat the milk and slowly stir it into the mixture. Heat to a boil, but stir carefully to keep lumps from forming. Add salt, pepper, and a pinch of freshly grated nutmeg. Remove from heat. Beat the egg yolk and stir in a tablespoon of the sauce. Then pour the egg into the rest of the sauce. Bring to a high heat, stirring constantly, but do not boil.

Lightly grease a baking dish of suitable size (about 12 x 7 x 2 inches). Make a layer of sautéed eggplant on the bottom of the pan, then add a layer of the meat mixture. Repeat the layering once, ending with a layer of eggplant. Evenly spread the sauce over the top. Bake for 45 minutes or until brown on top. Serve with lots of salad, bread, and plain yogurt.

Montana Venison Loaf

Since venison tends to be dry, this recipe needs shortening of some sort. I specify bear fat (which was often used by pioneers, and is very good) but it can be hard to come by these days, so beef suet, lard, or bacon drippings may be substituted. Modern health foods experts will, however, recommend that the measure be cut in half and that vegetable oil be used instead of animal fat.

>2 pounds ground venison
>¼ cup rendered bear fat (or Crisco)
>1 large onion, minced
>¼ cup green pepper, minced
>1 cup rolled oats
>2 chicken eggs, beaten
>1 cup tomato or V-8 juice
>½ cup catsup
>¼ cup prepared horseradish
>1 teaspoon dry mustard
>salt and pepper to taste

Preheat the oven to 375 degrees. Melt the fat in a cast-iron skillet. Sauté the onion and green pepper for 5 or 6 minutes. Mix all the ingredients except for the catsup. Put them into a greased pan or Pyrex dish of about 10 x 6 inches and shape into a loaf. (I also use my 10-inch cast-iron skillet, which, of course, has an ovenproof handle and cooks nicely.) Spread the catsup evenly on top. Bake for 1 hour, but check for doneness after 40 minutes. (A good deal depends on individual ovens and their thermostats.) Feeds six to eight.

Venison Loaf with Sauce Topping

This recipe goes nicely with any lean meat and is ideal for low-fat ground venison because it has some binders (eggs and oatmeal) in it.

The Loaf
2 pounds ground venison
2 chicken eggs, nicely whisked
1 cup rolled oats (regular oatmeal)
1 cup milk
1 medium onion, chopped
1 tablespoon catsup
1 tablespoon Worcestershire sauce
1 teaspoon salt
½ teaspoon pepper

The Sauce
1 can tomato paste (6-ounce size)
1 tablespoon prepared mustard
1 tablespoon dark brown sugar

Preheat the oven to 350 degrees. Whisk the eggs in the bottom of a large bowl and mix in the other ingredients. Grease a meat loaf pan and spread the mixture evenly into it. Mix the topping and spread it over the loaf. Bake for an hour. Eat with mashed potatoes and green beans. Serves six or more, depending on what you've got to go with it. Leftovers are good the next day.

Sloppy Joes for Bill

One day not long ago my wife was busy working on her doctoral dissertation and I was pressed to meet a tight deadline for a cooking column for *Gray's Sporting Journal.* My son, home from college for a few days, offered to cook supper. He wanted some sloppy joes, he said, so he went shopping to get the makings. He brought home a large can of sloppy joe mix, a pound or two of ground meat, and a package of buns. It was very tasty, and the same easy dish can be prepared with ground venison. Just follow the directions on the can. In short, brown the venison, pour in the contents of the can, and pour the results over opened hamburger buns, face up. If you want to make an improvement, brown a finely chopped onion or a couple of cloves of minced garlic along with the venison. If you want something special, pull up a handful of small wild onions and sauté them (using part of the green tops) along with the meat.

Here's a recipe if you want to start from scratch instead of buying a canned sauce.

> 2 pounds ground venison
> 1 pound ground pork
> cooking oil
> 1 large onion, chopped
> 1 cup catsup
> 1 cup tomato or V-8 juice
> 1 cup shredded cheddar cheese
> 1 tablespoon chopped parsley (optional)
> salt and pepper to taste

Heat a little oil in a skillet, then brown the meat and onion. Pour off the excess oil. Add the other ingredients and simmer for an hour. Serve on open buns with french fries and large dill or sweet pickles.

Variation: If you've got fresh wild mushrooms at hand, add a cupful either diced or sliced.

Venison Hobo

This recipe makes a complete meal, allowing one hobo for each person. These can be made to order, leaving out whatever isn't wanted or adding garlic or other vegetables as requested.

> ¼ pound ground venison
> 1 medium to large potato, cut into ½-inch slices
> 1 carrot, cut into strips lengthwise
> 1 medium to large onion, cut into ½-inch slices
> ½ stalk of celery
> mushrooms, garlic, etc. (optional)
> salt and pepper

Preheat the oven to 325 degrees. Shape the ground venison into a patty and place it in the center of a large sheet of heavy-duty aluminum foil. Add potatoes, carrot, onions, celery, mushrooms, and garlic. (Peel and scrape the celery, then cut it into 3-inch pieces.) Salt and pepper to taste. Fold the foil over and crimp the edges. The idea is to form a tight seal to hold in the steam. Put the hobo in the center of the oven. After 45 minutes, check to see if the potatoes and carrots are tender. If not, seal again and cook for a few more minutes.

This is a good camp recipe because a complete meal can be prepared in a package. The hobo can be cooked in a Dutch oven or on a grid over an open fire or coals, but do not cook it too close to a hot fire because the bottom may burn before the rest gets done.

Venison Burgers with Crumbs of Real Bread

A New York editor who scribbled all over one of my book manuscripts tried to change a recipe in which I had called for soft bread crumbs. I said that such bread crumbs could be made by pulling apart plain or sourdough white bread, either fresh or stale. He in turn said that bread crumbs aren't made from real bread.

Nonetheless, I say that bread crumbs bought in a can are too dry for use with many venison recipes.

> 2 pounds ground venison
> 1 cup real bread crumbs, soft
> 2 chicken eggs
> 1 medium onion, chopped
> ½ cup red wine
> salt and pepper

Shred the bread rather finely and do not pack it tightly into the measuring cup. Whisk the egg in a large bowl and mix in all the other ingredients. Shape the mixture into patties about ¾ inch thick and either broil them in the oven or cook them on a grill. Do not overcook. Grease your rack so that the burgers will be less likely to stick and tear when turning. For best results, grill between two racks or in a burger basket that can be flipped over. Serve in hamburger buns with your choice of trimmings. Try Pickapepper sauce.

Open-Faced Venison Burgers

This tasty dish is easily prepared and makes a nice lunch on a cold day. I like it with potato chips and a big dill pickle.

> 1½ pounds ground venison
> ¼ cup prepared chili sauce
> ¼ cup prepared horseradish
> ¼ cup prepared mustard
> ¼ cup Worcestershire sauce
> salt and pepper
> melted butter or margarine
> 8 hamburger buns

Mix venison, chili sauce, horseradish, mustard, Worcestershire sauce, salt, and pepper. Spread mixture onto hamburger bun halves, getting about the same amount on each. Preheat the broiler and brush each burger lightly with butter. Broil about 6 inches from the heat for 10 minutes, more or less, depending on the exact distance from the heat. (Remember that open-faced burgers are not turned.) Sample a burger for doneness before serving.

Venison Hash

This easy dish makes a complete meal, and I like it for lunch on a cold day, along with plenty of coffee, hot bread, and green salad.

> 1 pound ground venison
> 1 medium onion, diced
> 1 can tomatoes (16-ounce size)
> ½ bell pepper, diced
> 2 tablespoons cooking oil
> ½ cup long-grain rice
> ½ cup water
> 1 teaspoon chili powder
> 1 teaspoon salt
> ¼ teaspoon black pepper

Preheat the oven to 375 degrees. Heat the oil in a skillet and brown the venison, onions, and green pepper. Stir in the other ingredients, mixing well. Put the mixture into a greased baking dish with a cover. Bake for 45 minutes. Serve hot.

Venison Burgers

These burgers should be cooked and eaten on the spot. If you intend to freeze the ground meat, leave out the seasonings and oil. These can be added when you are ready to cook.

> 2 pounds venison
> 1 tablespoon canola oil
> 1 teaspoon garlic or celery salt
> ½ teaspoon black pepper
> ½ teaspoon dry mustard

Mix all of the ingredients and run the meat through a grinder. Shape the ground meat into four patties of ¼ pound each. Grill the patties over coals or broil the burgers in the kitchen oven for a few minutes until they are medium-rare to medium. Do not overcook. Serve on large buns with your choice of trimmings.

Note: These burgers can also be cooked in a skillet. Simply add a little margarine to prevent sticking and cook on medium heat for a few minutes on both sides until done.

Juicy Venison Burgers

This recipe works best with a hinged rack that can be flipped over instead of having to turn each burger. I got the recipe from a book on American Indian cookery and I recommend it highly, although I fail to see the Indian connection with some of the ingredients. Maybe they got the hog bacon from the settlers.

> 1½ pounds ground venison
> bacon
> 3 green onions, minced with part of tops
> ¼ cup dry red wine
> 4 large buns, toasted
> salt and pepper to taste

Build a hot fire of wood or charcoal and let it burn until you have good coals. Shape the venison into four patties about 1 inch thick. Cut some bacon strips to cover each patty, and then place the patties, bacon side down, into the bottom of the grilling basket. Then place bacon strips on top of each patty. Close the basket, lock it, and grill 3 or 4 inches from the coals for 2 or 3 minutes per side. The venison should be medium rare at about the same time the bacon looks ready to eat. Place each patty on a toasted bun, top with chopped green onions, and sprinkle with 1 tablespoon of red wine, salt, and pepper. Top the bun and serve.

Note: This recipe can also be used with the kitchen broiler, placing the meat very close to the heat source. The oven door should be left open while broiling, which permits you to use the long-handled grilling basket.

Venison and Mozzarella Burgers

Here's a recipe that my son Jeff, a burger-and-potato boy, says is the best ever. I came up with it while writing this book and experimenting with ways to cook ground venison without all the beef suet and pork fat that is normally put into it. The recipe calls for chopped garlic in oil. This mix is available in 2-ounce jars, usually at the produce counter of the supermarket. The jar keeps for a long time in the refrigerator and the garlic is very easy to use, although garlic lovers may tend to add too much of it! If you have a supply of home-grown or wild garlic, it's easy to make your own jar of garlic. Just peel the cloves, chop them with a chef's knife, put them into a jar, and cover them with olive oil. Keep the jar in the refrigerator and dip out the garlic as needed, allowing ½ teaspoon or so for a clove. (Actually, cloves of garlic vary considerably in size, so that the measure is not exact.) If you don't care for garlic, chop a spring onion or two.

>   ground venison
>   mozzarella cheese
>   minced garlic in oil
>   cooking oil
>   salt and pepper to taste
>   potatoes (cooked separately)

Allow about ⅓ pound of meat for each burger and sprinkle in some salt and pepper. For each burger divide the mix into two equal sections and shape into flat patties about ½ inch thick. Onto one patty, sprinkle a little mozzarella cheese and some garlic, making sure that the garlic and cheese don't spill over the edges. Next, carefully place the other patty atop the cheese and garlic. With your fingers, pinch the edges of the two patties together, binding them. Heat a little oil on a griddle or in a skillet. Cook the burgers until done, turning once. Usually, 5 or 6 minutes on each side will be about right on medium-low heat. (It's best to test one before serving. I usually cut my own in half to see if the inside is still red.) Serve these burgers in large buns, spread with catsup, mayonnaise, and other condiments. Even lettuce is good. Jeff likes them with mayonnaise and mustard, put onto a plate with two large dill pickles and plenty of my fried potato slices, made as follows.

Heat a little oil on the grill or in the skillet (the burgers and potatoes can be cooked in separate skillets or, better, on a large rectangular grill). Slice the potatoes about ¼-inch thick. (I don't peel them, but suit yourself.) Cook on both sides until browned. Spread the slices on a brown paper bag to drain, then sprinkle on one side with salt and mild paprika. A slice of tomato or two will round out the meal.

These burgers and potatoes are very filling and make a good meal in camp, especially if a large griddle is available. Drippings from the breakfast bacon can be used to cook both the burgers and potatoes.

Venison-Burger Steaks

This recipe is one of my favorites for venison burger, partly because the gravy makes it moist and tasty. The measures are for two steaks.

> 1½ pounds ground venison
> 1 tablespoon canola oil
> margarine for pan frying
> 1 medium onion, chopped
> 2 cloves garlic, minced
> salt and pepper to taste
> flour-and-water paste (1 tablespoon each)

Mix the meat, oil, salt, and pepper. Shape the meat into two steaks that will fit into your skillet. Melt a little margarine (or butter) in a skillet and cook the steaks for 5 minutes on medium heat. Turn carefully and cook for 5 minutes more. Remove the steaks and put them on a brown grocery bag. Add a little more margarine to the skillet, if needed, and sauté the onions and garlic for about 5 minutes. Stir in the flour-and-water paste with a wooden spoon. This will quickly become gravy. Add more water as needed. Stir in salt and pepper to taste. Carefully return the steaks to the skillet and simmer for 5 minutes. Top the steaks with gravy and serve with bread and vegetables or a freshly tossed green salad.

Variation: Add a few sliced mushrooms along with the onions and garlic, or add a can of mushroom soup instead of making gravy.

Easy All-American Chili

If you've got a pound or so of ground venison and want to fix a quick pot of chili, purchase a package of chili seasoning. These are sealed envelopes of spices and other seasonings, usually sold in a large display of similar mixes for gravies, sloppy joes, meat loaves, and so on. You'll probably find one mix for hot chili and another for mild. Suit yourself.

Read the back of the package and purchase the other stuff (except for the meat) required to complete the magic formula—usually a can of tomatoes and a can of red kidney beans. When you get home, pour a little oil into a large skillet and brown some ground venison. (Most of the packages will call for 1 pound of ground meat, but I like a little more. Usually, ground meat has lots of fat in it, but of course venison is quite lean and needs a little oil in the skillet.) When the meat is nicely browned, add the other ingredients, stir, cover, and simmer as directed on the package. Serve in bowls with crackers.

If you want to improve this recipe without going to lots of trouble, add a chopped onion and a minced clove of garlic to the meat when you brown it. For something truly different, don't cook the chopped onions. Serve them raw atop the chili in each bowl. This works best with mild onions, such as Vidalias.

FOUR

Venison Roasts

The important point to remember about venison roasts is that they should not be overcooked with high, dry heat. If they are, the meat will be dry, tough, tasteless, and difficult to swallow. The best venison roasts (or at least the most dependable) are cooked in a crockpot or by some other method of long, slow cooking over low heat, either immersed in liquid or enclosed in a steam-proof container. Any venison that is baked in an oven without being well covered or that is cooked over coals or under a broiler will quite likely be overdone or be charred outside and raw inside. A roast cooked in a covered roasting pan is partly cooked by steam instead of dry heat. Also, when a roast is cooked slowly in a stove-top Dutch oven with a tightly fitting dome-shaped lid, it is partly cooked by steam and also benefits from the "self-basting" effect, which is brought about by the fact that the steam condenses on the lid and drips down on the meat. Some of the cast-iron lids have little tits that help drop this condensation evenly. In my opinion, such a Dutch oven, if used on very low heat, is one of the best ways to cook venison roasts. It's almost as good as a crockpot.

Unless you are cooking on very low heat, the best bet is to insert a good meat thermometer into the center of the roast, making sure that it does not touch a bone. Check it from time to time. In an oven, the roast should be in the center. On a grill, it should be cooked by the indirect method; that is, cooked on one side of a covered grill with the heat on the other side.

Of course, some of the new silo-shaped smokers with water pans can be used to great advantage in cooking venison roasts

47

because they take advantage of slow, moist cooking. But there are wide differences among cookers, so instructions from the manufacturer should be followed. Again, the size and shape of the roast make a difference, so the only reliable guide is still a meat thermometer properly inserted into the meat. I recommend an internal temperature of 135 degrees for venison roasts, provided the meat sits for a few minutes before it is carved. This temperature is what I consider to be medium rare.

The problem, of course, is that venison is a lean, firm meat that has no fat marbling in the tissue like beef does. It also tends to be tougher than beef. Many cookbooks and experts recommend that venison be "barded" or "larded" to make it juicier, as explained below.

Larding and Barding: Larding is accomplished by inserting thin strips of salt pork or bacon into the meat with the aid of a large larding needle made especially for this purpose. Although I agree that larding a venison roast is a very good idea from a purely culinary standpoint, I don't think that many readers of this book will have a larding needle on hand—and I doubt that one can be found easily in most places. I've never seen one in a store—or in a kitchen, for that matter. They have declined from practical use in direct proportion (I feel) to the amount of fat in our cattle and pork. Even though the amount of fat in beef and pork may now start to decline, the larding needle isn't likely to make a comeback simply because lard and other animal fats are now generally believed to be unhealthy and of coronary consequence.

Nevertheless, it is still possible to obtain larding needles, and the same effect can be achieved by making slits in the roast and stuffing them with pieces of beef or pork fat. I do this from time to time but, frankly, I think the slits drain out lots of juice from the meat, offsetting the advantage of larding in the first place. If you do lard a roast, insert the needle with the grain. Then, when the meat is sliced across the grain, no piece will have a long streak in it.

Barding is similar in intent to larding, is much easier, and requires no special equipment. Usually, it involves wrapping the meat with strips of bacon or salt pork or, sometimes, putting such strips inside rolled roasts. One of my favorite roasts, for example, is made by sandwiching strips of bacon between two boned shoulders, then rolling and tying the meat.

Frankly, I like larding and barding. One of the best roasts I've ever eaten was cooked inside the fatty skin from a smoked pork ham. Still, the modern cook should consider the widely held opinion that animal fat isn't good for people.

Larding needles are still used by some knowledgeable chefs, but these days, lard or other fat is usually pumped into the meat with needles, along with liquid smoke, various preservatives, and other chemicals. Anyone who wants such a needle should check with the firms that deal in meat-processing and sausage-making equipment. Personally, I have never liked the idea of injecting anything into what I eat, but this is common practice these days and most "cured" hams purchased at the supermarket are pumped full of water and other stuff. If you want to try injecting venison roasts, remember that vegetable oil (peanut or canola) is generally held to be less harmful than animal fat.

Meat Thermometers: If a piece of prime venison is properly butchered, duly hung, and cooked to perfection, it really doesn't require barding or larding to be succulent. The main thing is that it should not be cooked too long. Overdone roast beef is tough and hard to swallow; venison gets to that point more quickly because it has very little fat.

A rare or medium-rare venison roast, on the other hand, is moist enough and usually tender. For best results, it should be sliced thinly against the grain. Also remember that hot venison is usually better than cold, so a roast should be eaten shortly after it comes from the oven. On the other hand, the British are fond of cold boiled venison served with a sauce. Boiled venison—or, better, venison cooked in water below the 212-degree mark—is usually more moist than baked venison.

Before getting to a few recipes, let's consider the various kinds of venison roasts, some of which are more juicy and tender than others.

NECK ROASTS

The neck of whitetail and other venison is ideal for cooking as a roast, and its meat is usually tender and moist. On the other hand, it doesn't slice as prettily as other cuts, and it is bony. I usually serve it when we have no formal guests, when gnawing at the table is permissible.

If you don't have any greens on hand, or don't care for them, simply put the neck into a pot. Add a package of onion soup mix and a little water, cover tightly, and simmer for 2 or 3 hours. Potatoes and other pot roast vegetables may be added, along with water to almost cover.

Necks may also be cooked to advantage in a crockpot, if they fit. Moose and elk necks should perhaps be cut in half and treated as separate roasts, and giraffes (which make excellent eating and which were at one time hunted for food and sport by African horsemen) would of course provide several neck roasts. In any case, fit the neck into the crockpot and add a little seasoning and ½ cup of water. Cover and cook on low for 8 or 9 hours. If you want a complete meal, add potatoes, onions, and other vegetables at the outset. I sometimes pour in 3 or 4 cups of water and add 1 cup of wheat berries or ½ cup or so of pearl barley.

SHOULDER ROASTS

The front legs of a deer contain tasty meat. The whole leg and shoulder can be removed easily with a good knife. With the deer hanging from the hind legs, push down on a front leg with your left hand and start a cut at the armpit, working in close to the back-bone. The leg is attached by a muscle-and-blade assembly, not by a ball and socket, so that the whole front leg can be removed without cutting through a bone.

After the leg is removed, the shank should be cut off and used in a way discussed under bony parts. The rest can be cut into a blade roast and a leg roast, but both of these will be small and rather bony, at least on the average whitetail. The best bet is to bone out the meat, roll it, and tie it with cotton twine. The best way, I think, is to cut into the blade end, following the natural divisions of the meat, working down to the bone, and proceeding along the bone. Try it. Remember that the meat will be pretty jagged when boned and flattened, and will be much wider on the blade end. Nevertheless, shape the meat and roll it, tucking in the ends and tying it. If the roast doesn't hold together, try again. If it looks hopeless, cut the thing into stew meat, and try again with the other leg. Practice makes perfect.

One of the best roasts is made by putting two boned shoulders together and tying them. Try sandwiching strips of bacon or salt pork between the meat before you roll it. Such a roast from a good-sized whitetail will weigh 7 or 8 pounds, if you are careful and skilled, but most people will end up with plenty of stew meat and meaty soup bones in addition to the roast.

Easy Venison Roast

This recipe makes a succulent and tasty roast without the aid of a meat thermometer, but don't cook it too long. Using a slow (not too hot) oven gives more leeway, so that timing is not as critical. Although this recipe can be prepared with any roast of suitable size, I like it with a boned and rolled shoulder roast.

>1 rolled shoulder roast, 3 or 4 pounds
>2 slices of bacon
>1 envelope of onion soup mix
>salt and pepper
>2 cloves of garlic

Preheat the oven to 250 degrees. With a sharp, thin knife, such as those designed for filleting fish, poke holes straight into the roast at two well-spaced points. Insert the garlic. Put the roast onto a flat sheet of heavy-duty aluminum foil. Grind or pound the onion soup mix to a powder. (I usually do this with a meat mallet while the mix is still in the package.) Add some salt and pepper and coat the roast with all the mix. Drape the bacon over the top of the roast. Fold the aluminum foil up lengthwise and crimp the edges, forming a tight seal. Put the roast into the center of the oven with the seam side up. Cook for 2½ hours. Carefully open the top and test for doneness. The roast should be medium-rare, with the inside pink and moist. If it is not ready, reseal and cook for another 15 minutes or so. Carefully remove the roast from the foil, and save the juice for serving over the meat slices.

Variation: If you prefer thick gravy, pour the juice into a skillet and thicken with a paste of flour and water. The last time I tried this recipe, I used thin slices of salt pork instead of bacon. It was delicious.

Note: If you bone and roll your own roast shortly before cooking, the garlic and bacon (or salt pork) can be put inside. If your meat cutter has boned and rolled the roast, put the bacon on the outside.

RIB ROAST

The backbone along the rib section of deer and similar animals contains very little tenderloin, but two strips of good meat run along the top on either side. On beef, these strips are the popular rib eye steaks or "prime rib." The backbone of larger animals is sometimes split and the halves of the rib section can be cooked as roasts. Of course, the whole cut can be cooked as a roast without splitting, but it will contain the backbone and will be difficult to carve. In any case, the rack of ribs is best removed with a hand or meat saw.

If you butcher your own meat, I would suggest that you cut the rib eye away from the backbone and cook it much like tenderloin or loin chops. If you've got an electric meat saw, try making rib chops from the rear end of the rack.

THE SADDLE AND THE BARON

The saddle contains the two loins and the two tenderloins, making it generally the most valuable part of the animal. It is the section of the backbone between the last set of ribs and the rump. Some hunters will remove the tenderloins while field dressing the deer (as I recommend), reducing the saddle somewhat. Others will cut out the tenderloins and loins, opting for chops or cutlets, or perhaps a long, slender roast of loin. Still others will have the saddle sliced into steaks, which is best done with a meat cutter's band saw.

The saddle can be cooked whole, as a roast. It's an oblong piece that's relatively easy to spit securely and fits nicely over larger outdoor grills. It can be cooked successfully on the patio, especially with a good rotisserie. Any good marinade and basting sauce can be used. I like to baste with bacon drippings, bourbon, and black pepper. The main point is not to overcook. The meat can be quite brown outside but inside it should be rare or at least medium-rare. A meat thermometer can be inserted from either end and pushed toward the center of the loin, being careful not to touch the bone. The saddle from an average whitetail will cook on a patio grill-and-spit rig in about 1½ hours, but a meat thermometer is the best guide. (Also consult the manual that came with the spit. It probably won't have directions specifically for venison, but any information about cooking a saddle of lamb will be pretty close.)

The baron, a term usually applied to beef, includes the saddle and the two hind legs. It is too large for most kitchen stoves and patio grills, but it can be cooked over coals in a long open pit. It must be secured to a rack or spit. It's easier to lash it to a rack shaped like a stretcher, with handles on both ends. Two people can tote it or turn it during cooking. The only foolproof advice that I can give is to keep it a good distance from the heat and turn it from time to time. Allow at least 4 hours to cook it. The danger, of course, is that the outside will cook to a crisp while the inside is still bloody.

Many patio cooks like to add smoke chips to the fire when cooking a saddle or baron. I prefer to cook over wood coals instead of charcoal or gas because the wood smells better to me and provides enough smoke. But that's just one man's opinion.

A saddle can also be cooked in the kitchen oven. It can be difficult to find the right container for a saddle, and I usually put it between two sheets of heavy aluminum foil, then seal the edges with double folds. Before sealing, I put in some peeled onions, vinegar, several cloves of garlic, and perhaps a little gin, which imparts the flavor of juniper berries. Then I cook the meat half a day at 250 degrees. Well before eating, I open the foil and cut into the loin, testing for doneness. Medium-rare is ideal, but this method uses steam if the foil is closed tightly, so that overcooking doesn't ruin the meat like dry heat does.

James Beard's Roast Saddle of Venison

There is some flank meat on venison, extending down and just under the hide, from the loin. Sometimes the loin section is cut in half and the flank on that side is rolled around the larger part (or under it) and tied. The flank meat on both sides can also be rolled around or under the entire saddle. Here's a good recipe for the latter from *The Complete Book of Outdoor Cookery* by James A. Beard and Helen Evans Brown.

"Trim and wipe a saddle of venison, lard it well, then roll the flank under the saddle and tie securely. Spit for balance and roast over a moderate fire until the meat thermometer reads 135 to 140 degrees. This is pinkly rare. If desired, a baste of olive oil and Italian vermouth may be used during cooking. Serve with mashed turnips combined with an equal part of mashed potatoes, and with string beans and mushrooms."

RUMP ROAST

If the word *rump* requires explanation, let me say that this rather large roast comprises the good meat between the loin and the leg. On larger venison animals, especially elk and moose, it can easily be divided into two or more roasts. The rump roast from whitetails goes nicely in one piece and makes good pot roasts. The rump roast can also be left attached to the hind leg for a really large chunk of meat. Butchering the rump roast is discussed briefly under Leg Roasts.

For recipes, see the suggestions under Pot Roast, or try my favorite method of cooking this cut, which follows.

Rock Salt Rump Roast

This recipe has been adapted from my book *Good Vittles,* and I highly recommend that you try it with a rump roast, which is of irregular shape and easy to mound over with rock salt. If you want to try my rock salt method of cooking a roast, purchase at least 5 or 6 pounds of ordinary ice cream salt. Preheat your oven to 450 degrees. Select a roasting pan large enough for the roast, with plenty of room all around. (I usually use an oven-proof ceramic dish that is attractive enough to put onto the table.) Line the bottom of the pan with an inch of rock salt. Pepper the roast all around, then carefully insert the thermometer. Place the roast onto the salt, turning it so that the thermometer sticks straight up. Slowly pour salt around the roast until all the meat is covered with at least ½ inch of it, then put the pan into the center of the preheated oven. Cook for ½ hour, then start checking the thermometer from time to time. Cook until it reads 130 degrees, then remove the roast from the oven. It can rest for a while, but should be served hot.

I always leave the roast encased in the salt when I put it onto the table. My guests watch as the salt is cracked off ceremoniously, usually by tapping it with the blunt end of a table knife until the mound cracks. I then meticulously pull the segments off in small pieces. Any remaining salt can be brushed off with the hand. Then the meat is transferred from the pan to a serving platter.

LEG ROASTS

Many people (even some butchers) saw through the backbone after the loin section has been removed. This gives a large chunk of meat that contains the legs, the rump, and part of the back. It's better, I think, to cut off the leg without the aid of a saw. This can be accomplished with a sharp knife. Start at the base of the tailbone and cut along the backbone as closely as possible, down into the meat to the point where the leg is attached with a ball and socket. Then the knife can be worked through the joint, helped along by working the leg back and forth and wrestling with it a little. Before long, the whole leg flops over and you can finish the job quickly. The first time you do this, you will probably leave quite a bit of meat along the backbone. This can be trimmed off and used as good stew meat or in gameburger, or it can be cooked on the bone with soup.

The shank is usually cut off the leg with a saw and used for stew meat, or cooked whole. After the shank has been removed, the leg (including the rump roast) can be cooked whole, or the whole can be reduced to parts. The rump part attaches to the leg with another ball and socket and can be cut off with a knife by carefully following the natural divisions of the meat.

After the rump is removed, you'll have the leg proper, which is often cut into round steaks, with a circle of bone more or less in the center. These steaks are difficult to cut in uniform thickness unless you have a professional meat saw. Some people, including myself, usually separate the leg into three segments. This is a natural division of meat, and the muscles are attached to one another with tissues. These separate muscles can be treated as small roasts or be cut into steaks or cutlets, as discussed in other chapters.

Also, the whole leg, or ham, can be treated as a large roast, with or without the bone. In my opinion, this is a difficult piece of meat to cook. But hunters somehow want to cook the whole thing—the bigger the better—and I am frequently ask how to do so. I always say, "Slowly, very slowly, with the aid of a good meat thermometer." That isn't what they want to hear, but I refuse to budge. The key is slow cooking, either on low heat or some distance from high heat. It's possible to cook such a large chunk on a rotisserie, but it's difficult to hold such a heavy piece of meat with most units for a long time, turn after turn; further, turning such a chunk of meat strains the unit's tiny gears and motor, so that breakdowns are not uncommon, especially if the meat isn't perfectly centered. Consequently, I recommend that the ham be cooked in the kitchen oven or by the indirect method on a large outdoor grill that has a cover. In either case, wipe the ham all over with vinegar and sprinkle it generously with black pepper. Insert a meat thermometer into the deepest part of the ham without touching bone. Fit the ham into a large oblong roasting pan and cover. If the lid won't fit, try heavy-duty aluminum foil, crimping the sides so that the moisture will stay inside. Turn the oven to 165 degrees and cook for two days. Be warned that your venison ham will be ruined if it gets too hot. Before following this recipe, test your thermostat with an oven thermometer and compare the readings.

If you want to cook outside, it's best to have a very large grill with a hinged cover. Build a charcoal fire in one end and put the venison (roasting pan and all, if possible) in the other end. Keep the fire small and barely burning. You need a really good temperature gauge on such a rig, but unfortunately most of the units marketed these days aren't very accurate. Open the vents just enough to keep the fire burning. Cook until the internal temperature of the venison ham reads 135 degrees, then let the meat sit for a while to finish cooking. Ideally, it should be pink through and through without dripping blood.

A third method of cooking a large chunk of meat—the best, in my opinion—is to build a hot fire over a pit in the ground. Coat the meat with prepared mustard and sprinkle with pepper, then wrap it in a clean burlap bag. Smear prepared mustard all over the burlap, then tie everything with a piece of cotton twine or wire. (I buy a gallon of mustard at a time and it is very cheap as compared with small jars.) When the fire burns down, place some of the coals out of the pit and some inside. Lower the ham onto the coals, then cover it with the coals from the ground. Next, fill the hole with dirt and make a mound over it. Let the ham cook all night. When you're ready to eat, carefully dig it out and peel off the burlap. It will be very tender and delicious.

All of the recipes above can be cooked in heavy aluminum foil, but it's hard to seal a large ham, especially if it is turned or peeked at from time to time. I think that the pit method works best without the foil, which keeps the flavor of the fire out of the meat. For the ultimate in flavor, wrap the meat in banana, ti, or agave leaves, or seaweed. Even cabbage leaves or large collard leaves can be used, if you can keep them around such a large piece of meat.

POT ROAST

This term, as I use it, doesn't designate a specific cut of meat. Instead, it's any good-sized roast that fits nicely into a pot. Of course, the pot itself can be most any container of suitable size, including the old-fashioned black iron ones that were suspended over a fire or coals. I usually use a stove-top Dutch oven with a tight lid, but even the lid can be omitted if you want to fill the house with plenty of good aroma, or forgot to bring the lid when you packed for camp. If you cook without the lid, be sure to keep an eye on the water level, unless you like your roast burned on the bottom.

Pot Roast of Venison

This recipe contains the basic procedure for cooking most pot roasts and can be modified considerably, as in the next recipe, simply by adding vegetables that seem fitting. I usually make this recipe in a stove-top Dutch oven with a rack or trivet on the bottom, but any pot will do if it has a tight lid. Any sort of venison roast will do if it fits into the pot.

> 3- or 4-pound venison roast
> 2 tablespoons cooking oil
> 1 onion
> salt and pepper to taste
> flour

Salt and pepper the roast, then roll it in flour, covering all sides. Heat the oil in the Dutch oven and brown the roast, turning frequently. Remove the roast and scrape up any bits of flour that have stuck to the bottom. Put a low rack in the Dutch oven. (If you don't have a rack, build one by first splitting a carrot into four pieces lengthwise.) Add the sliced onion and a cup of water. Put the roast onto the rack, cover tightly, and simmer for 2 or 3 hours. Turn the meat a few times, and add a little water if necessary. When the roast is tender to the fork, put it on a serving platter and take the rack out of the pot. Increase the heat and cook and stir the liquid until you have a thick sauce, tasting and adding a little salt and pepper if needed. To serve, slice the roast thinly across the grain and top with gravy. If you want a sauce that is a little more unusual than ordinary gravy, add a tablespoon of red currant jelly to the liquid.

This recipe is, of course, a good one to cook in camp, especially if you have a gas stove that can be turned down to low for long cooking. If you've got a sassafras tree near camp, make a rack with peeled green limbs or even roots. This method gives the roast and gravy a spicy flavor that is like no other. Some people like to drink a cup of sassafras tea from time to time, and some old-timey cooks knew that sticking a few splinters of sassafras root into a roast would serve as a spice. Try it.

Pot Roast Dinner

Follow the preceding recipe until the roast has cooked for an hour. Add 2 cups of water, turn the roast, and cook for another ½-hour. Increase the heat and add the following:

> 8 small red new potatoes
> 8 small onions, whole (golf ball size)
> 2 cloves garlic, chopped
> 1 carrot, sliced into wheels
> 1 stalk celery, chopped
> fresh parsley sprigs (optional)
> 8 ounces fresh mushrooms (optional)

Cover tightly and simmer for 40 minutes, or until the vegetables are tender. To make lots of gravy, melt 2 tablespoons of butter in a small skillet and stir in 2 tablespoons of flour until it starts to brown nicely. Transfer the meat and vegetables to a heated serving platter. Increase the heat under the Dutch oven and bring the liquid almost to a boil. Stir in the roux, adding more water as needed, to make a thick sopping gravy. Serve the meat, vegetables, and gravy with hot, fluffy biscuits.

Easy 5 Pot Roast

Here's a recipe that's easy to remember and easy to cook, making it a good one for camp if you've got fresh vegetables.

> 5-pound venison rump roast (or smaller)
> 5 whole potatoes
> 5 whole carrots
> 5 whole onions
> cooking oil
> flour
> salt and pepper

Heat a little oil in a pot or Dutch oven. Salt and pepper the roast, then dust it with flour. Brown on all sides. Add a cup of hot water, cover tightly, and steam the roast for 3 hours. Turn the meat from time to time and add more water if needed. After it is more or less tender, add all the vegetables and another cup of water, along with a little more salt and pepper. Bring to heat, cover, and simmer for another 30 minutes, or until the vegetables are done. Put the roast and vegetables onto a heated serving platter. Make gravy with the pot liquid, thickening with flour if needed. Pour the gravy over the venison and vegetables and serve.

Note: Other vegetables can be added, including celery, turnips, or mushrooms.

Sauerbraten

This old dish is a good example of using a marinade as a part of the recipe, not merely as a soak. Any good venison roast will do for sauerbraten, but I prefer a boneless piece. A rump roast is fine.

> **The Roast**
> 1 venison roast of about 4 pounds
> flour
> ¼ cup cooking oil

The Marinade
1½ cups red wine vinegar
1 cup red wine
1 cup water
2 large onions, sliced
½ lemon, sliced
1 tablespoon sugar
1 tablespoon salt
10 cloves
10 peppercorns
1 tablespoon mustard seeds
5 bay leaves

The Gingersnap Gravy
½ cup gingersnap crumbs
2 cups pan liquid
½ cup sour cream

Crush the peppercorns and mustard seeds. Add to the other marinade ingredients in a large, non-metallic bowl. Put the roast into the marinade, turn it, and refrigerate for two to four days. Turn the meat at least once a day.

When you are ready to cook, remove the roast and pat it dry with paper towels. Save the marinade. Dust the meat with flour, coating all sides. Heat the oil in a stove-top Dutch oven and brown the roast on all sides. Quickly strain the marinade and add the liquid to the pot. Bring to a boil, reduce heat, cover tightly, and simmer for 3 hours or until the meat is tender. Remove the meat from the pot and put it on a serving platter. Measure out 2 cups of pan liquid. (If necessary, add a little water to make 2 cups.) Put the liquid back into the pot and increase the heat. Stir in the gingersnap crumbs and heat to boiling, whisking as you go. Reduce heat and whisk in the sour cream, being careful not to boil the gravy at this point. Pour some of the gravy over the roast and serve the rest in a gravy bowl.

Baking Bag Roast

At one time, some people cooked fish and meat in a brown bag, but these days, I am told, bags from grocery stores, or at least those made from recycled paper, may explode in the oven or catch on fire. In any case, the modern plastic bags designed especially for baking in an oven are easier to use. I recommend them for cooking venison roasts. Even though it's difficult to tell when a roast is done to perfection, the method allows for more error than dry-heat cooking. Here's a recipe to try.

> 3- or 4-pound venison roast
> 1 tablespoon flour
> 1 can tomato sauce (8-ounce size)
> 1 rib celery, chopped
> 1 tablespoon Worcestershire sauce
> salt and pepper to taste
> noodles or rice (cooked separately)

Preheat the oven to 350 degrees. Dump the flour, salt, and pepper into a 24-by-18-inch baking bag and shake. Put the bag into a baking pan of suitable size at least 2 inches deep. Trim the roast and place it into the bag. Add the tomato sauce, celery, and Worcestershire sauce. Tie the bag and punch a few holes in it, according to the directions on the package. Put the pan into the midsection of the oven and cook for 2 or 3 hours, depending on the exact size of the roast and the accuracy of your thermostat. If in doubt, try the "fork tender" test after 2 hours: Stick a long two-tined fork through the top of the bag and into the roast. If it seems tender, chances are that it is ready. Medium-rare is best. If you think it is done, remove the pan from the oven and let it sit for a few minutes. Slit the bag and put the roast on a heated serving platter. Make gravy from the drippings. Pour some of the gravy over the roast and serve the rest over rice or noodles.

Leftover Venison Roast

Not long ago, we had some leftover venison roast, but it wasn't enough to feed our family of four. Besides, even roasts that are perfectly cooked (on the rare side) tend to dry out when reheated. Checking the refrigerator, my wife found a short link of smoked venison sausage. Remembering that the Cajuns sometimes use smoked sausage in jambalaya, we made a quick decision. The flavor of venison roast and smoked venison sausage was memorable. Here's my recipe.

> 1½ pounds leftover venison
> ½ pound smoked venison sausage
> 2 cups hot water
> 2 beef bouillon cubes
> 8 green onions with tops
> 8 ounces fresh mushrooms
> 1 tablespoon parsley
> 1 teaspoon salt
> ½ teaspoon pepper
> rice (cooked separately)

Cut the sausage into wheels about ½ inch thick and dice the leftover roast. Dissolve the bouillon cubes in the hot water. Slice the mushrooms. Chop the onions, including the lower half of the green tops. Grease your stove-top Dutch oven (or large frying pan with cover) and brown the sausage. Add the venison, bouillon mixture, mushrooms, onions, parsley, salt, and pepper. Bring to low boil, reduce heat, cover tightly, and let simmer for an hour. Mix 2 or 3 cups of cooked rice into the dish just before serving. Eat with hot French bread and tossed salad. Serves four.

FIVE

Variety Meats

The American cowboys enjoyed a dish called son-of-a-bitch stew. It consisted of more or less equal parts of liver, heart, sweetbreads, lights, tongue, and the marrow gut. The "lights" refer to the lungs and the "marrow gut" is the tube that connects the two stomachs of cud-chewing animals, such as cattle, deer, elk, and others. Typically, the stew was made by the bullcook on the trail.

A similar stew can be successful in a deer camp, unless the hunters are too squeamish to enjoy cowboy fare. Proceed by cutting all the parts into cubes. Put a little grease into a Dutch oven or iron pot and brown a chopped onion or two and a clove of garlic if you have it. Add all the chopped parts; a diced green pepper, if you have it; and some salt. Cover with water and simmer until the parts are tender.

When on the range alone, a cowboy probably wouldn't trouble to make such a stew. He would simply wrap the marrow gut around a stick and roast it over coals from the campfire. The nomadic peoples in the Sahara Desert also wrap entrails on a stick and roast them, and the Greeks make a kabob in which variety meats are strung on a skewer and wrapped with entrails.

The venison parts called sweetbreads and the lights are not commonly eaten these days, but they are still edible. Also, whitetail testicles are just as good as those of a sheep, and the same can be said of moose and elk. In fact, moose fries are eaten in Canada.

For the sake of those readers who are weak of stomach, perhaps I had better come forth quickly with recipes for more common victuals, such as venison liver. Culinary sports can, of course, skip the first few recipes and move forward to more exotic fare.

LIVER

Far too many sportsmen ignore game liver, which is among the most nutritious of meats. Almost all liver from healthy animals can be eaten and is tasty if handled properly, although some experts warn that polar bear liver may contain too much vitamin A for human consumption. I have also eaten liver from birds such as coot and from fish. The liver of the ordinary eelpout (burbot) is considered to be a delicacy in some quarters. I've also eaten liver from large turtles, and I'll have to rate liver of the Florida softshell (which grows up to 40 pounds) as high on my list.

In any case, venison liver is not only very good but is also easy to obtain and prepare. During field dressing, merely cut the liver out with a pocketknife, put it into a plastic bag, and keep it cool, preferably on ice. It's best to eat the liver right away, and it is often cooked in deer camp. The whitetail doesn't have a gallbladder, so there's nothing around the liver to taint the meat, unless, sometimes, the animal was gut shot and didn't drop right away. Be sure to try venison liver in your favorite recipe or try some of the dishes below.

Venison Liver with Onions

Liver and sautéed onions are a classic combination. Sometimes the ingredients are cooked separately and added at the last minute, or they can be cooked together in a large skillet. I prefer the latter method, and I usually add some mushrooms and bacon. I don't normally measure the ingredients, but two medium or large onions will do for one deer liver. Try about 8 ounces of mushrooms and four strips of bacon.

> venison liver
> bacon (or peanut oil)
> onions, sliced
> mushrooms, sliced (optional)
> flour
> salt and pepper

Fry the bacon in a large skillet until crisp. Remove and drain. Slice the liver into strips no thicker than ½ inch. Salt and pepper the strips, then shake them in flour. Heat the bacon drippings (or peanut oil) and sauté the onions and mushrooms. Remove with a slotted spoon. Turn the heat up and quickly brown the liver for 2 or 3 minutes. If you fry the liver too long, it will be tough and tasteless. Add the onions and mushrooms, and salt and pepper to taste. Simmer for 2 or 3 minutes and serve with the bacon.

Rumaki

American cooks of Oriental inclination commonly make this dish with chicken livers, which are fine. I like it with venison liver, and, I confess, I also eat it for lunch, not merely as an hors d'oeuvre.

> venison liver
> thin bacon
> water chestnuts (canned, sliced)
> sake

Marinate the liver and water chestnuts in a little sake for an hour or so. When you are ready to cook, cut the liver into 1-inch cubes. Put a piece of liver together with a slice of water chestnut, wrap them with a short length of bacon, and pin with a toothpick. (The bacon should overlap by about ½ inch, just enough for a good hold.) Grill on a stove top or indoor grill or broil in the oven. Better, cook the kabobs over charcoal or wood coals. As a rule, the liver is done when the bacon is crisp.

Variation: I cook a similar dish with onions and mushrooms instead of water chestnuts. Venison liver kabobs can be made in this manner and served over rice. This also makes a good camp recipe, using a green stick as a skewer. As an alternate camp method, don't cut the bacon; merely string it up ribbon fashion, going over and under pieces of liver, mushrooms, and onions. Hold the stick and rotate it or turn it often while cooking. Puffballs are good when cooked in this manner with liver and bacon.

Venison Liver with Wine

Cut a deer liver into ½-inch slices. Salt and pepper each lightly, then shake in flour. Melt ½ cup of butter in a skillet and brown the liver. Add 1 cup of chopped onions, a minced clove of garlic, and ½ cup of dry red wine. Cover and simmer for about ½ hour, stirring from time to time.

Broiled or Grilled Venison Liver

Liver can be broiled in the oven successfully, or better yet, it can be grilled over charcoal. The trick is to avoid long, direct cooking over high heat. It's always best to serve it rare or medium-rare. One trick, however, is to cook it with bacon, which adds both moisture and flavor. This can be accomplished by wrapping pieces of liver in bacon and grilling like kabobs, as in the recipe for rumaki. Another method is to use two racks or an adjustable grilling basket, as in the following recipe.

> 1 pound venison liver
> 8 strips of thin bacon
> ½ teaspoon dried oregano
> ½ teaspoon dried basil
> salt and black pepper to taste

Build a wood or charcoal fire in the grill. Slice the liver into ½-inch-thick pieces and dust on both sides with the seasonings. Arrange the slices tightly onto one of the broiling racks. Cover with four strips of bacon. Put the other rack atop the bacon and turn the works over. Remove what is now the top rack and put the remaining bacon onto the liver. Put the rack back on. When the coals are hot, grill the liver on both sides, about 4 inches from the heat, until the bacon looks ready to eat. Be warned that bacon drippings will cause a mighty fire in your grill if you aren't careful. I like to have a large grill with lots of surface area so that the liver can be moved about when a flare-up occurs. This requires constant attention for about 8 minutes.

The same recipe and method can be used for broiling in the oven, directly under the heat, but no more than 4 inches away. The two racks should, of course, be small enough to fit atop the regular oven rack.

Venison Liver Flambé

If you want a more formal recipe for venison liver, slice it into pieces ⅓ inch thick. Salt and pepper to taste and shake in a bag with flour. Heat a little butter or margarine in a skillet and brown the liver well on both sides, for a total of about 5 minutes. Do not overcook. Heat a little brandy and pour it over the liver. Ignite with a kitchen match. (Use about ¼ cup of brandy for each batch of liver, assuming that you are using a 10¾-inch skillet.) Put the liver on a heated platter. Swish up the pan juices and pour them over the liver. Serve hot. I like this dish with rice pilaf and plenty of vegetables or salad.

Easy Italian Venison Liver

Cut the liver into slices ½ inch thick. Put the meat into a bowl and pour in a little Zesty Italian salad dressing. Marinate for 20 or 30 minutes, or longer. Drain the liver and roll each piece in grated Parmesan cheese. Brown in a skillet, using about ⅛ inch of olive oil or a little butter. This dish is best on the rare side; do not cook too long. Serve hot.

LIGHTS

The lungs of various animals are eaten in some areas, often under the name of lights. I've eaten them myself, cooked together with liver, under the name of Liver n' Lights, but, frankly, I have never cared for them and I therefore don't have much personal experience to offer the cook. Perhaps the lights that I have eaten were not prepared correctly or were not "beaten" adequately. In short, they were too "light" for me, owing, I suppose, to the air inside the tissue.

In any case, venison lights have been eaten in various countries in times past. Anyone who wants to try them may proceed without fear of dire consequences, provided that the lights are removed during the field-dressing operation and kept cool. I would suggest that the lights be beaten with a meat mallet and cut into pieces for use in a stew, along with other meat.

VENISON HEART

The heart of most wild animals is usually larger, pound for pound, than that of domestic animals because wild animals run more, pumping more blood. Since the heart is basically a muscle, it is usually tough, especially that of game. Generally, the heart from any large game should be boiled or steamed for a long time before it is eaten. It can, however, be grilled quickly and eaten rare.

Of course, the heart should be removed from the innards as soon as possible, but it is not quite as perishable as the liver or sweetbreads and should not necessarily be cooked right away. I like to keep the heart on ice, upside down, for several days. It should, however, be split and trimmed right away. It's best to split it lengthwise, starting at the big end. If frozen, the heart can be kept for several months, or longer if it is frozen in water.

Venison Heart with Gravy

The measures below will cook one venison heart, which will usually feed two people if they aren't too hungry. Hearty eaters should prepare lots of rice or biscuits to eat with the gravy. Cook more than one heart, if available.

> 1 venison heart
> cooking oil or margarine
> flour
> 1 cup water
> 1 cup milk
> 1 large onion, chopped
> 8 ounces fresh mushrooms, sliced
> 1 bell pepper, sliced
> salt and pepper to taste

Split the heart open from end to end and cut out the sinew and blood vessels. Slice the meat against the grain into strips about ⅜ inch thick. Salt and pepper to taste and shake in a brown grocery bag with flour. Save the bag and dump the excess flour into a bowl. Heat about ¼ inch of oil in a large skillet and quickly brown the strips. Drain on the bag. Sauté the onion, bell pepper, and mushrooms in the skillet for 5 or 6 minutes, then remove with a slotted spoon and drain on the bag. Pour off excess grease, but leave a little. Add 2 tablespoons of flour and brown on low heat for a few minutes. Mix 1 cup of milk and 1 cup of water and slowly stir it into the roux. Pour and stir until you have a thin gravy. Add the heart and the sautéed vegetables. Cover and simmer for 2 hours on very low heat. Do not boil. Stir from time to time with a wooden spoon and add more of the milk-and-water mixture if needed. Do not allow the bottom to burn. Taste and add a little salt and pepper as you go. Serve with rice or mashed potatoes.

Venison Heart Sandwich

This recipe is best cooked in simmering water for a long time. You can also use a pressure cooker.

> 1 venison heart
> 2 bay leaves
> 2 cloves
> salt and pepper
> rye bread
> prepared mustard or horseradish

Cut the heart in half lengthwise and trim off the sinew and blood vessels. Put it into a pot, cover with water, and add bay leaves, cloves, salt, and pepper. Bring to a boil; reduce heat, cover, and simmer for an hour, or until the heart is tender. Chill the heart in the refrigerator, then slice it very thinly. Spread fresh rye bread with mustard or horseradish, or both. (I like brown Creole mustard, or my own homemade mustard.) Place several thin slices of meat in each sandwich and serve them for lunch with potato chips and dill pickles, or potato salad. Venison tongue also makes a good snack, served on small thins of rye.

KIDNEYS

The kidneys from whitetail and similar animals are found along the backbone and are sometimes attached to it after the guts have been removed during field dressing. The kidneys can be removed easily and are well worth the effort. Of course, they are dark, kidney-shaped organs, rather small for whitetails of normal size. Although the kidneys from a small deer will not feed an entire family, they can be cooked and used as a side dish, or as a meal for one. I like them in venison-and-kidney pie (or beef-and-kidney pie), in which the exact ratio of kidney to other meat is not critical. See the venison-and-kidney recipe in chapter 10 or try the following.

Grilled Kidneys

Whitetails and other deer have tasty kidneys that can be cooked over a campfire or patio barbecue. Cut them into bite-size pieces and thread them onto a stick or skewer. Baste with melted butter and grill close to hot coals for 2 or 3 minutes. Turn, baste, and grill for 2 or 3 minutes on the other side. Do not overcook. Baste again, add salt and pepper to taste, and eat. Because whitetails have rather small kidneys, I consider these to be an appetizer to sample while the stew is cooking over the campfire, or as a conversational side dish to more usual fare.

Grilled kidneys also make a good hot lunch for the hunter lucky enough to bag his deer in the morning. They can be wrapped in bacon and cooked on a forked stick over a campfire.

Sautéed Kidneys Bradford Angier

I got this recipe from *Gourmet Cooking for Free,* written by Bradford Angier, and I have used it with great success. I sometimes cook

71

this dish just for myself and eat the whole thing. If you have two deer, double the recipe and invite someone to share it with you.

>1 set deer kidneys
>butter
>1 tablespoon minced onion
>4 tablespoons sherry
>salt and pepper
>cayenne pepper

Slice the kidneys thinly. Heat the butter in a small skillet on medium heat. Sauté the kidneys for 4 minutes, adding salt and pepper to taste. Put them on a heated serving dish. Sauté the onion for 3 or 4 minutes. Add the sherry and sprinkle lightly with cayenne pepper. Cook and stir until the mixture thickens a little. Pour the sauce over the kidneys and eat. I like this dish with steamed cauliflower, sliced tomatoes, and hot bread.

TONGUE

The tongues of reindeer are highly prized in Northern Europe, and those of whitetail and other venison are just as good. Smoked tongue of caribou and buffalo are considered to be delicacies, and at one time, buffalo were killed only for their tongue, which was in high demand in restaurants in Chicago and points east.

It's best to cut out the tongue during field dressing, unless you are going to cook the whole head. With a sharp knife, merely cut out the tongue at the base. It is not as perishable or as delicate as some of the other variety meats, but it should be kept cool. Aging tongue is not required, although they keep nicely in the refrigerator for a few days. They also freeze well.

The only problem with a whitetail tongue is that it is too small to feed more than one or two people. A moose tongue will feed a whole family. In any case, one of my favorite ways to serve tongue is to boil it and serve on crackers or rye thins, as follows.

Tongue Appetizers

 1 deer tongue
 water to cover
 1 medium onion, chopped
 2 bay leaves
 1 teaspoon pickling spice
 1 teaspoon salt
 ½ teaspoon red pepper flakes

Wash the tongue, trim it, and cover it with water. (Some people scrub the tongue with a brush, but I don't think this is necessary, since it is usually peeled after cooking.) Add the onion, spices, red pepper, and salt. Bring to a boil, cover tightly, reduce heat, and simmer for 2 hours or longer. (Tongues from mule deer or very large whitetails may require longer simmering; as a rule, the tongue is done when a fork can be inserted and removed easily.) Let the tongue cool in the liquid so that it will absorb some of the spice flavor, then chill. Serve it thinly sliced (crossways) on crackers with Creole mustard, or slice and use it as sandwich meat.

Apricot Tongue

Here's a good venison tongue recipe that I borrowed from Lue and Ed Park's *The Smoked-Foods Cookbook*. They recommend that the tongue be simmered for 2 or 3 hours in seasoned water or broth, as in the preceding recipe. Then it is smoked for an hour or so and basted once with the sauce described below. After smoking, it is eaten with the sauce, made as follows.

 1 package dried apricots
 ¾ cup catsup
 ⅔ cup brown sugar, packed
 2 teaspoons grated fresh ginger root
 1 tablespoon soy sauce

Mix all ingredients in a pan and heat until the apricots are soft. Use part of the sauce to baste the tongue as it smokes, then eat the rest with sliced tongue.

BRAINS

Brains are very tasty. The only problem with venison brains is getting to them. A butcher or meat processor can merely cut the skull in half lengthwise and the brains can be removed. If you don't have access to an electric meat saw, try an ax or sledgehammer. In any case, remember that the brains should be removed fairly soon after the animal drops. They can be eaten right away because aging isn't necessary. There are good recipes for lamb and calf brains that will work with venison brains. The best bet, however, is to scramble them with eggs, as discussed in chapter 12.

Venison brains are also delicious fried. Chill the brain and cut it into 1-inch cubes with a thin filleting knife. Heat some cooking oil in a skillet. Salt and pepper the squares and roll them in flour. Fry them until they are golden brown. If you have a lemon, squeeze a few drops of juice on each serving.

STOMACH

It may not sound too good, but the stomach of grazing animals contains some good meat and salad. That's right. Some primitive peoples remove the contents of the first stomach and eat it. Reportedly, it tastes like salad greens sprinkled with a little vinegar. If you don't develop a taste for the contents, remember that the stomach itself is good eating, and is often called tripe. Also, the whole stomach is sometimes stuffed and eaten, as in haggis, or used as a cooking vessel.

Venison Tripe

Tripe is the stomach lining of animals such as cattle, deer, and moose. Most cookbooks contain recipes for it. I am fond of menudo, a Mexican soup-like dish made with tripe and various ingredients. There are dozens of recipes. One of my favorites contains lye

74

hominy, chili powder, and an onion or two. This is a wonderful combination, especially when prepared with homemade lye hominy. Other recipes call for garbanzo beans (chickpeas), tomatoes, fresh coriander, and even pig's feet.

The ingredients listed below are more or less my own selection and include venison sausage. The key is to get a fresh stomach from the deer and clean it right away. I don't know how this *should* be done correctly, but I merely slit the stomach open and turn out the contents, wash the meat inside and out, and cut it into 1-inch squares.

> 3 pounds tripe
> 1 pound venison sausage, sliced
> 1 large onion, chopped
> 3 large ripe tomatoes, chopped
> 2 tablespoons fresh parsley, chopped
> salt and pepper
> water
> cooking oil

Place the tripe in a pot, cover with salted water, and boil for 3 hours or until tender. Drain. Heat a little oil in a skillet and fry the sausage. Drain. Sauté the onion. Drain. Then fry the tripe until browned. Add the sausage and onions to the skillet, along with the tomatoes and parsley. Stir and heat through. Reduce the heat, cover tightly, and simmer for 30 minutes.

Note: In parts of Mexico, menudo is believed to be a remedy for hangover and is often eaten for breakfast after a festive night.

Haggis

Haggis is a traditional dish in Scotland and is made with red deer (elk) as well as with lamb or mutton. The stomach of the animal is washed, turned inside out, washed again, and stuffed with a little chopped meat, liver, heart, lights, and kidneys, along with spices and Scotch whiskey. Usually, the various meats are first boiled and then stuffed into the pouch. Then the whole works is boiled for about 2 hours. It swells and must be pricked here and there to avoid bursting and spilling out the contents. It is served whole, with a spoon. At a deer camp, I once questioned a little red-headed American Scot about haggis, and he said it is all a damned lie!

In any case, the idea is not peculiar to Scots. According to Herodotus, the ancient Scythians were fond of stuffing a mare's stomach with meat or parts of the same animal. They used the stomach as a vessel, boiling or simmering the contents over a fire made with bones.

Also, Plains Indians used buffalo stomach as a cooking utensil. Instead of stuffing it, however, they opened it up a bit and stretched it out over the fire, suspending it from posts. They put water into the stomach, using it like a pot, and boiled meat in it. After being used several times, the stomach itself was eaten and a fresh one was used as a pot.

In any case, if you want to try a haggis from deer (or elk, moose, or pronghorn), take out all the parts mentioned above, along with the kidneys and the sweetbreads, if you can find 'em, and add a pound or two of diced meat from the neck or shoulder. Boil until everything is tender. Cool the meat and then chop each piece. Add a couple of large onions, chopped, and a cup or two of rolled oats. Stir in ½ cup of Scotch whiskey and 1 cup of water, plus salt, pepper, and other spices, such as thyme and powdered mustard. Add a little water and mix with your hands. Turn the stomach, stuff it, and sew it up with cotton twine and a large needle. Place the haggis into a pot and cover it with water. Bring to a boil, reduce heat, and simmer for an hour or two. After cooking for 30 minutes, prick a few holes in the stomach so that it won't burst. When you are ready to feast, put the haggis onto a platter, remove the twine, and dig in with a large spoon.

According to Angus Cameron and Judith Jones in the *L.L. Bean Game and Fish Cookbook,* haggis is traditionally served with "neeps and tatties," or turnips and potatoes, sometimes mashed together.

FRIES

Hungry peasants, culinary sports, and good ol' boys the world over have eaten the testicles of sheep, hogs, and other animals, often as "mountain oysters" or "fries." The French call them *animelles,* and I understand moose testicles are popular among French Canadians. In any case, there are a hundred recipes, but I think most Americans will want to keep this delicacy simple. As the saying goes, "Anything that can't be fried ain't fit to eat," so, if you've got a young buck and feel frisky, try the following.

Remove the fries during field dressing and keep them cool. Skin them and cut them into quarters, lengthwise. Coat them with a mixture of lemon juice and olive oil and let them set for an hour. Dry them, sprinkle with a little salt and pepper, and shake them in flour. Then sauté in hot butter or cooking oil until they are nicely browned. Eat while hot. It is customary to garnish the fries with parsley sprigs and serve them with tomato sauce. Catsup will do if you don't have tomato sauce.

SWEETBREADS

I have eaten sweetbreads that I purchased in the supermarket, and I found them to be very good. Most recipes recommend that they be marinated or simmered for a few minutes in water and a little lemon juice, then used in various ways. They are wonderful when cubed, dusted with flour, and fried. Also, try them scrambled with eggs. They are quite close to brains in texture, and I think that the recipes are more or less interchangeable. But I confess that I've never eaten sweetbreads from a deer or other game animal. The problem is in knowing what's what among innards, and the confusion isn't straightened out in most books on the subject.

I can tell you that there are two kinds of sweetbreads, those that come from the pancreas and those from the thymus. Other than that, you're pretty much on your own.

BLOOD

Modern American hunters may have mixed feelings about this topic. For generations, we have been told that we should bleed deer well if the meat is to be fit to eat. Not many years back, the experts were saying that the animal's throat should be cut. These days, most of us don't bother with trying to bleed the animal, knowing that a lung shot and quick field dressing are better and quicker. Still, most of us associate blood with a strong gamy taste and wouldn't dream of eating it, although much blood is still left in the meat no matter how the animal is butchered. Perhaps we should remember that blood from domestic animals is used even today in sausages and puddings. Further, some European recipes call for blood to be used in the sauce or gravy. *Civet de Chevreuil,* according to my old edition of *Larousse Gastronomique,* calls for blood of the deer to be used in the sauce, saying that it can be replaced by hare's blood. Culinary experimenters should perhaps be warned, however, that after adding the blood the dish should not be heated above 158 degrees, at which point blood coagulates and the mixture curdles.

Perhaps I should also point out that many peoples in the past have used blood for food without killing the animal. The warrior horsemen of the Asiatic steppes, for example, would take extra animals with them on long journeys. Each day they would draw a little blood from a different animal, thereby getting nourishment without having to stop to cook or to build a fire, the smoke from which could give away their location.

ENTRAILS

People all over the world use intestines of hogs, sheep, and cows as sausage casings. They can also be consumed in other ways, usually after thorough washing inside and out, but sometimes whole and with the contents intact. Anyone who has eaten sardines, for example, will have noticed that they are merely beheaded and packed, guts and all. So anyone who has eaten canned sardines or raw oysters shouldn't criticize others who like the following selection. It's merely a matter of size.

Chitterlings

I have mixed feelings about the name of this delicacy. Calling them "chitterlings" in my part of the country would first bring a frown of confusion that would be followed by a knowing nod, indicating that they knew the term as "chitlins" and accepted a slight speech impediment. Normally, the term is applied to cooked hog entrails, but these parts of other animals are also edible.

If you want to try venison chitlins, cool the intestines as soon as you can after field dressing. Strip out the contents, then turn the intestines inside out and wash them several times. The normal procedure is to slit the intestine from one end to the other and then cut them into pieces, about 1 inch wide and 2 inches long, but they can also be cooked in doughnut shape. After washing and cutting them, soak them overnight in cold salted water, using 1 teaspoon salt to each quart.

When you are ready to cook, cover the chitlins with water in a pot and bring to a hard boil. Reduce heat and cook until tender. (Be warned that some people don't like to smell boiling chitlins, so perhaps good ol' boys can complete this step outside the house.) Drain. Roll in finely ground white cornmeal (water-ground style) or flour and fry in deep fat until golden brown. Delicious.

Innards on a Spit

There are several convenient recipes for lumping all the innards together, such as the cowboy stew and haggis. The complete patio chef or camp cook may prefer a modern version of an ancient Greek recipe. Make kabobs by cutting the heart, liver, kidneys, and sweetbreads into cubes and stringing them on a skewer. Strip some of the intestines and wash them inside and out. Wrap a suitable length of intestine around the cubes and grill as usual, basting with a sauce made of olive oil, salt, pepper, and oregano.

SIX

Bony Parts

One well-known outdoor writer has talked about leaving the bones of a deer in the field. I think he's crazy. Of course, leaving all the bones, along with the hide and the less obvious variety meats, will reduce the weight of a deer considerably and is therefore the thing to do if transportation is a problem. A 150-pound whitetail on the hoof can be reduced to 100 pounds of pure meat. I might add that boning out the meat also reduces the freezer space required to hold a deer or a moose and simplifies the packaging. If at all possible, however, the hunter would do well to consider keeping and using all the bony parts, as discussed in this chapter.

RIBS

One of the tastiest parts of a deer is usually thrown away or fed to the dogs. People who have learned to barbecue deer ribs would prefer if a deer were all ribs.
—Ed Wuroi, *The Maine Way*

After the front shoulders have been cut away from the backbone, the ribs can be removed easily with a saw. A meat saw is preferred, but most any sort of hand saw will do. The first step is to cut through the "breast bone" or cartilage that connects one set of ribs to the other. (This can be accomplished with a heavy knife or meat cleaver, but a saw works faster.) Then each rack of ribs can be removed by merely cutting through the ribs along the backbone. These sections of ribs can be cooked whole or the rack can be sawed in two lengthwise. These pieces in turn can be cooked whole or be divided into smaller pieces by merely cutting the meat between the ribs. The ribs on top, where they connect to the backbone, will have more meat than the bottom and are sometimes considered to be rib chops; sometimes these are sliced uniformly between the ribs so that they can be grilled or broiled easier. The lower ribs are best compared to spareribs and have very little meat, but what's there is good and worth the effort.

Some people who have to butcher the meat afield leave the ribs with the rest of the bones. In this case, if there is time, the hunter should at least cut out the meat with a sharp knife and save it as stew meat. Working down one rib and up the other, this doesn't take long.

If you take your deer to a meat processor, be sure to discuss ribs with him and decide what you want. Ribs don't require long aging and can be cooked right away. Consequently, they make a good choice for cooking in camp if you are in the backcountry for several days and have a deer or two hanging. But remember that the deer should be skinned before the ribs are removed, a task that some hunters prefer not to do in camp. Some people even leave the skin on for a week or longer while the deer hangs in cold storage, which is what I recommend.

In any case, here are a few suggestions for cooking ribs.

Venison Ribs and Easy Dumplings

Venison ribs tend to be sparse, especially from a small whitetail, so be sure to allow about a pound or more for each hearty diner. The measures in this recipe can be adjusted easily to feed more people.

> 4 pounds venison ribs
> ½ cup cooking oil
> 1 large onion
> 1 tablespoon Worcestershire sauce
> flour
> salt and pepper
> water
> flour tortillas or dumpling dough
> 2 or 3 hard-boiled chicken eggs

This dish works best in a stove-top Dutch oven or a large skillet with a lid. Salt and pepper the ribs, then shake them in a bag with a handful of flour until they are coated. Heat the oil and brown all the ribs that will fit into the Dutch oven or skillet. Brown in more than one batch if necessary. Brown the onions along with the last batch. (Heat a little more oil if necessary.) When all the ribs are nicely browned, pour off the excess oil. Put all the ribs into the pot and add the Worcestershire sauce. Cover with water and turn the heat to high. Cut the tortillas into strips, allowing an 8-inch tortilla for each pound of ribs. (The tortillas can be made at home, but I usually buy them at the supermarket. I have also used cornmeal tortillas for dumplings, as well as homemade dumpling dough. Also, ready-made biscuits can be made into drop dumplings by merely pinching off pieces and dropping them into the liquid. Suit yourself.) Drop the tortilla strips or other dumplings into the pot one at the time. Bring to a boil, reduce heat, cover, and simmer for an hour and a half, or until the meat is very tender. Slice the eggs and stir them gently into the broth during the last 15 minutes.

This recipe is a good one for camp if you butcher a deer and have ribs on hand. They are good fresh and do not require curing.

Baked Rib Barbecue

Grilling and broiling ribs are discussed in another chapter, but remember that ribs can also be baked in the kitchen oven. It's best to cut them into pieces and allow at least 1 pound per person.

> 4 pounds venison ribs
> ½ pound bacon
> 1 medium onion, chopped
> flour
> 2 cups barbecue sauce
> ½ cup apricot jam
> salt and pepper

Preheat the oven to 325 degrees. Heat a skillet and fry the bacon until it is crisp, then put it on a brown bag to drain. Salt and pepper the ribs, then shake them in a bag with a little flour. Brown the ribs a few at a time and put them on the bag. Sauté the onion for a few minutes. Arrange the ribs in a greased baking dish. Put the barbecue sauce, crumbled bacon, and jam into the skillet with the onions, mixing and heating through. Pour the sauce over the ribs and bake for 1½ hours. Eat while hot—with your fingers, of course.

Easy Rib Barbecue

Preheat the oven to 325 degrees. Put 3 pounds of venison ribs into a baking pan of suitable size. Mix 2 cups of barbecue sauce with a 12-ounce can of cola (I prefer Classic Coke). Cover the dish tightly with aluminum foil and bake for 2 hours.

Skillet Ribs

I love to eat venison ribs, and I also love to cook in a large skillet, making this recipe one of my favorites. It's from Mrs. Sherman Clement, as quoted in *The Maine Way*.

"Cook 1 large chopped onion slowly in ½ cup margarine. Add 2 tablespoons vinegar, 1 cup catsup, 1 teaspoon chili powder, 1 cup water, 2 tablespoons Worcestershire sauce, 1 tablespoon dry mustard, 1 tablespoon brown sugar, 1 teaspoon salt, ½ teaspoon pepper, ¼ teaspoon garlic salt, or to taste. Place [venison] spare ribs in this sauce and simmer 2 to 3 hours or until done."

SHANKS

The hooves and lower legs of the deer and similar game are usually sawed off at the knee and discarded after the animal has been skinned. I recommend this practice, especially with the hind legs, which contain the tarsal glands. (Never try to cut these glands out.) Saw off the whole lower leg at the knee and discard it; it is all bone and hide. Then the bony piece called the shank can be cut off from the lower end of the "ham."

The shanks contain some good meat that is usually cut off and thrown into the stew meat or burger meat pile. But they can be cooked whole in recipes that call for long simmering, and I highly recommend cooking them all day in a crockpot with a little salt and pepper and some vegetables. As a rule, a shank of a normal deer will be enough for one person. Although I don't offer a recipe specifically for venison shanks, I wouldn't hesitate to try any recipe for lamb shanks from a dependable family cookbook, if it called for long simmering over low heat.

NECKS

As stated in the chapter on roasts, a venison neck is one of the more succulent parts. It should never be left in the field. If necessary, the meat can be cut off and rolled into a small roast. This is accomplished by cutting around the neck at the head and the breast, as if to remove it entirely. Then make a lengthwise cut down to the bone and start working around the neck. The result will be a slab of meat, easy to roll and tie. The meat can also be cut off in pieces and used for stews, or ground into gameburger.

If you want to remove the whole neck for use as a pot roast, cut all around close to the head. Find the right spot in the spinal linkage and you can cut and twist the head free with only a pocket-knife. Then work on the other end the same way. When you reach bone, a saw will come in handy but isn't necessary if you've got a big knife or a meat cleaver.

BONES

We have discussed neck bones, rib bones, and backbones. Now it is time to take in all bones, including those from the shoulder and hind leg that are left when the meat is removed as roasts or cutlets. The bones can contribute to some of the best eating, especially if you are not very skilled at "boning" a shoulder, thereby leaving some meat attached here and there, as I do. What's left of the saddle after the loins and tenderloins have been cut out makes the best eating of all when cooked down in a soup or stew or with greens such as turnips, collards, dandelion, dock, beets, and other leafy plants of the garden and field. In any case, try venison bones in a good soup recipe, and I trust that the following will be just right.

Best Venison Bone Soup

I cook this recipe with bits of meat and rich stock obtained from the bony parts of a deer. Often, I'll start the recipe during the butchering process. In a large pot, boil some of the bones in water with a couple of bay leaves. For best results, the bones should be cracked or sawed in half. After boiling for a couple of hours, I remove the bones and pull off any meat that is left. Then I put 2½ cups of the stock into a 5-cup freezer container (suitable for the microwave), and fill it with cubed venison. The container is put into the refrigerator to cool, and is eventually frozen unless I intend to cook soup within a few days. This procedure allows you to have some good soup mixes ready but doesn't fill up the freezer with bones.

For soup stock, I'll often keep the boiling going for several hours, using neck bones, backbone, leg bones, and even ribs. To see that it's worth the trouble, try the following recipe, which can be made for less than $3, if you've got the soup bone stock.

> 5 cups venison bone soup stock with meat
> ½ cup barley
> 1 package frozen soup vegetables (16-ounce size)
> 1 can tomatoes (16-ounce size)
> 8 ounces fresh mushrooms (optional)
> 1 teaspoon chopped chives
> ½ teaspoon crushed basil leaves
> ½ teaspoon salt
> ¼ to ½ teaspoon pepper

Thaw the vegetables and the stock (with meat). Bring the stock to heat and add the vegetable mix, tomatoes, barley, mushrooms, chives, basil, salt, and pepper. Bring to boil, reduce heat, cover, and cook on low heat for an hour.

Venison Bone Marrow

Like blood, venison bone marrow is not highly regarded by most modern American hunters, and some experts say that marrow will taint the meat and should not touch it under any circumstances whatsoever. On the other hand, marrow is highly regarded by some gourmets, and in my opinion is wonderful stuff. American Indians also thought highly of bone marrow from buffalo and other animals, and in Africa the giraffe, which was at one time great game for horsemen, is highly prized for its bone marrow.

For marrow at its best, saw the bones into segments about 4 inches long. Cover them with water in a pan, bring to a boil, reduce the heat, and simmer for 10 minutes. While the bones are simmering or cooling down, whittle some marrow sticks, with which you push the marrow through. Eat it with a touch of salt, or plain. If you aren't serving guests, you might suck on one end while pushing on the other. If you've got enough for a mess, serve it on pan-fried toast. Also, marrow bones are often baked or cooked in the coals of a campfire.

In any case, marrow is a fatty, nutritious brain-like substance that has been enjoyed since prehistoric times. Even some animals eat marrow, and a smart buzzard in South America knows how to take the bones high into the air and drop them onto rocks to crack them open.

If you want to sample it but have mixed feelings, try a little scrambled in with eggs. You'll like it just as much as brains and eggs scrambled together. Remember, anyone who has eaten the half-round piece from the bone end of T-bone steaks and pork chops has already tasted marrow.

Bones and Greens

One of my favorite ways to cook neck bone and backbone is with greens such as turnips or collards, or a mix of turnips and mustard. Dandelion, dock, pigweed, and other edible wild greens also are good. The idea is simple. Put the neck bone into a large pot and add enough water to almost cover it. Then add salt and pepper.

Wash some greens and chop them. Fill up the pot and turn up the heat. When the water gets hot, the greens will wilt and more can be added. Simmer for 2 hours.

HEADS

The head contains some of the best variety meats, as discussed in the last chapter. The tongue is usually cut out and treated separately, and sometimes the brains are also removed after first splitting the head open.

At home, the whole head can be cooked in, over, or under the fire. When it is to be cooked in a pot, the head should be skinned and boiled until tender. The meat can then be pulled off and used in one way or another, as in head cheese. Use the nose and ears if you like them, and remember that the large bulb-like nose of a moose is a delicacy in some quarters.

The head can also be cooked in camp. A culinary sport by the name of C. E. Gillham once described in *Field & Stream,* how he and some Indians cooked a caribou head in the Yukon. They built a good fire and rigged a tripod over it. From the tripod they suspended the head and neck, hair and all, and cooked it for several hours. The hair burned off and the skin charred, but it was easy enough to scrape off. Underneath, the meat was tender and toothsome. Gillham said that the Indians gave him an eyeball—an honor—and reported that it might have been good with a touch of salt.

Of course, the head of whitetail and other venison can be cooked in the same way. The neck can be left on or removed, depending on how many people have to be fed. There is, however, no good way to divide the eyeballs equitably among three or more hunters.

At one time, some people in America cooked pig's head for making souse or headcheese, using the ears, nose, and other good parts, but the practice has declined. Even farmers buy meat at the supermarket these days. I guess that such eating has also declined in most other countries and that the trend will continue. But whole heads are still cooked in some areas, and lamb heads provide

87

something of a feast in the Middle East. There are numerous recipes, but one of the most primitive, and suitable for deer camp, comes from Turkey. First a roaring fire is built in a pit in the ground. When the coals have burned down, the head is put into the pit, facing Mecca, and covered with dirt. The next day, the head is taken out and the skin is scraped off, exposing the succulent meat. In some parts of the Middle East, it is customary to brush the animal's teeth before cooking the head.

SEVEN

Venison with Grains and Vegetables

The recipes in this chapter include some interesting "new" grains as well as some old favorites used in different ways. The first half of this chapter includes recipes for venison and grains, and of course, such common grains as rice figure into recipes throughout the book.

Vegetables can also be cooked to advantage with venison, as shown in the recipes in the last half of this chapter. Of course, a number of other recipes throughout this book also call for vegetables of one sort or another.

Venison and Wild Rice

I adapted this recipe from *The Art of American Indian Cooking*, and I highly recommend it not only for anyone interested in our native foods but also for anyone who likes healthy eating. Make sure that you have 100 percent wild rice instead of a mix. Wild rice makes excellent food for ducks and other wildlife and can be sown around and in beaver ponds and other marshes. Harvesting some of it for the table won't hurt a thing.

> 4 pounds of venison, cut into 2-inch cubes
> 1½ cups wild rice
> 2 quarts of water
> 2 medium onions
> 2 teaspoons salt
> ⅛ teaspoon black pepper (or a little red pepper)

Put the meat into a pot with the water and onions. Bring to a boil, reduce heat, cover, and simmer for 2 or 3 hours, or until the venison is tender. Wash the wild rice in cold water and add it to the pot with the salt and pepper. Bring to a new boil, reduce heat, cover, and simmer for 20 minutes. Remove the cover, stir, and simmer until most of the liquid has been absorbed by the rice.

Black Beans, Rice, and Venison

I have always enjoyed the combination of black beans and white rice, a dish that is sometimes called Christians and Moors in Cuba. Add some venison to the mix, along with a vegetable or two, and you have a complete meal.

> 1½ pounds venison, cubed
> ham bone with a little meat
> 12 ounces dry black beans
> 1 chopped onion
> water
> salt and pepper
> olive oil
> rice (cooked separately)
> toppings (see below)

Black beans don't have to be cooked quite as long as pintos; I allow 3 hours from start to finish. Put the beans into a Dutch oven or suitable pot. Add 4 cups of water and the venison, ham bone, chopped onion, salt, and pepper. Bring to a boil, cover tightly, reduce heat, and simmer for 2½ or 3 hours. Stir from time to time, adding a little water if needed (the bottom could scorch and ruin the whole pot of food).

About 30 minutes before serving, cook 1½ cups of long-grain rice and prepare toppings of your choice. Remove the ham bone from the beans and pull off the lean meat. Chop it and return it to the pot. At this point, you should have a moist mixture but not much liquid in the bottom. (If you've got too much liquid, cook a little longer with the lid off the pot.) Pour in a little olive oil and toss to make the black beans shine.

Mix the rice in with the beans and venison. Serve in bowls with fresh bread and toppings of your choice. If you've got several people at the table, it's fun to put out several bowls of toppings so that everyone can suit himself. Try mild onions chopped and chilled; ripe tomatoes, diced; bell peppers, diced (one green and one orange, mixed); shredded cheese; and thick sour cream. I like the toppings to be served cold, perhaps on ice, so that I get a combination of hot and cold along with the mix of flavors. With all of this, I like some hot, chewy bread, such as Italian, brushed with garlic butter.

Venison and Wheat Berries

The wheat berries used in this recipe are not cracked wheat. They are whole kernels with only the husk removed. Hard wheat is best. Various kinds of wheat berries are found in grocery stores as well as in health food outlets. Several mail-order sources also carry wheat and other whole grains. The hard wheat berries are wonderful in this recipe and give a texture that isn't available with cracked wheat. Wheat berries are also good for you.

I usually cook this recipe in a crockpot, but a Dutch oven or other suitable pot can also be used provided that the ingredients are simmered on very low heat for a long time.

>
> 3 pounds of venison stew meat
> 1 cup hard wheat berries
> 1 16-ounce package frozen stew vegetables
> 1 large onion, chopped
> 3 cups water
> 3 beef bouillon cubes
> 1 tablespoon dried parsley
> salt and pepper to taste

Put the wheat berries into a crockpot with the water. Add the venison, onion, frozen stew vegetables, bouillon cubes, salt, pepper, and parsley. Turn the crockpot to low and cook for 8 or 9 hours.

Venison and Burghul

In the Middle East, cracked wheat (called burghul or bulghur) is commonly cooked in dishes of lamb or camel. Antelope or other good venison can also be used in these dishes. There are thousands of suitable recipes, and the one below, which I adapted from Claudia Roden's *A Book of Middle Eastern Food,* is typical and one of my favorites. I use it because it is heavy on tomatoes (an American vegetable that has now been adapted all over the world). Burghul is available in many health food stores and increasingly in supermarkets. It's also available by mail. I cook the dish below with the aid of a cast-iron skillet and stove-top Dutch oven.

> 1½ pounds cubed venison
> 4 cups burghul (cracked wheat)
> 3 medium tomatoes, chopped
> 1 small can tomato paste (6-ounce size)
> 2 medium onions, chopped
> 2 sticks margarine or butter
> salt and pepper
> water

Melt 1 stick of margarine in a skillet and sauté the chopped onions for 5 or 6 minutes. Add the meat and brown slightly for 5 or 6 minutes, stirring in some salt and pepper to taste. Add the tomatoes and tomato paste. Cover with water, bring to a boil, reduce heat, and simmer for 2 hours, or until the meat is very tender. Add a little more water if needed.

When the meat is almost done, melt the other stick of margarine in the Dutch oven on rather high heat. Add the cracked wheat and stir fry for 10 minutes. Add a little salt, then add the meat and sauce from the skillet. Stir well, cover, and simmer for 10 minutes, or until all the liquid has been absorbed. Next, put an asbestos mat under the skillet and "steam" the mixture for ½ hour on very low heat. (Some people stretch a cloth over the skillet, then cover it. I seldom use the cloth or lid, preferring to stir the mixture while it steams, helping it along until it is plump and soft.) Good stuff.

Ms. Roden says that the dish can also be made with chicken instead of red meat, in which case the cooking time can be reduced. Try it also with a pheasant cock cut into pieces and cooked for about 1 hour.

Venison and Barley

To me, barley is one of the world's greatest grains, not for bread but for soups and stews. It is available in more than one form, but pearl barley is by far the most common and is used in this recipe.

> 1 pound venison, suitable for slicing
> 1 cup pearl barley
> 4 cups water
> 2 cups beef stock (or canned broth)
> 8 ounces mushrooms, sliced
> 1 carrot, thickly sliced
> 1 medium onion, sliced
> 2 cloves garlic, sliced thinly
> ¼ cup peanut oil
> salt and pepper

Put the barley into a pot and add the water. Bring to a boil, reduce heat, and simmer for 20 minutes. While the barley cooks, slice the venison very thinly. Heat the oil in a large skillet and stir-fry the venison for 3 minutes. Remove the meat and drain. Using the grease left in the skillet, sauté the onions and garlic for 3 minutes. Add the carrots and mushrooms and cook for 3 minutes. Drain the barley and add it to the skillet with the beef stock, salt, and pepper. Bring to a boil. Reduce heat, cover, and simmer for 20 minutes. Add the beef, stir, and cook for 2 or 3 minutes. Serve with hot bread, a huge tossed salad, and a dry red wine.

Venison and Whole-Grain Hominy Stew

The best hominy is homemade, using ashes from a hardwood fire. This is sometimes called lye hominy. It is also called whole-grain hominy because it is made from whole-kernel corn instead of pieces of corn (as in grits). But lye hominy is a lot of trouble to make and canned whole-grain hominy is available in most supermarkets. Fresh hominy may also be available in some areas, and dried hominy seems to be gaining in popularity and is very good. Dried hominy is usually soaked overnight, but I find that, like pinto beans, it can be cooked for hours with venison without prior soaking. (The recipe below calls for canned hominy, but it can be adapted to the dried kind.)

Hominy is often used in Mexican cuisine and is a standard ingredient in menudo (tripe) recipes and some other dishes. It was also popular with the Indians of the Southwest, who called it "corn without skin." It is still popular in the Southwest, and is often called *posole* or *pozole.* Hominy can be eaten in various ways, and is the basis for *masa harina,* the tortilla corn meal. This recipe is really for a dish that the Zuñi made with mild green peppers instead of hot red ones. I got the basic recipe from *The Art of American Indian Cooking,* an excellent work now available in paperback, but I left out the oregano and parsley. I also specify venison instead of lamb. Add the parsley (½ cup fresh, minced) and oregano (2 teaspoons) if you like. Dried juniper berries are available in the spice section at some supermarkets. They can also be picked from juniper trees and dried. They are used in quite a few game recipes and were apparently used as a seasoning by Indians of the American West. They are also used to flavor gin distinctively, and a little gin in turn can be used to advantage in some game recipes.

    3 pounds venison, cubed
    3 cans hominy (15½-ounce size)
    6 medium green peppers
    2 medium onions
    2 cloves garlic
    6 juniper berries, crushed
    salt and pepper to taste
    ¼ cup cooking oil
    flour
    water

Put the flour and meat into a bag and shake. Heat the oil in a stove-top Dutch oven and brown the meat, onions, and garlic, stirring and adding the crushed juniper berries as you go. (Actually, it will be difficult to really brown the meat in such a small amount of oil, but do the best you can, cooking and stirring on high heat for 7 or 8 minutes.) Add salt and pepper to taste. Add the hominy and liquid from the cans. Pour in 4 cups of water. Core and quarter the peppers, and add them to the pot. Bring to a boil, cover, reduce heat, and simmer for about 2 hours, or until the venison is tender.

Variation: If you can find dried hominy, be sure to try it. Use 1½ cups of dried hominy and double the water in the recipe above. (One cup of dried hominy makes about 3 cups cooked.) Dried hominy can be simmered for a long time without cooking it apart, which makes it a good choice for tough venison, scrawny Florida range cows, or Texas jackrabbits.

Venison and Triticale

Triticale, the world's first man-made grain, is a cross between wheat and rye. The name came from combining the scientific name for wheat *(Triticum)* with that of rye *(Secale)*. The result is a nutritious berry of good flavor. It is becoming more widely available and can be ordered by mail.

> 1 pound ground venison
> 3 cups beef broth
> 1 cup triticale berries
> 1 large onion, chopped
> 1 can tomatoes (16-ounce size)
> salt to taste
> ½ teaspoon red pepper flakes

Lightly brown the ground venison and onion in a skillet or saucepan of suitable size. Add the other ingredients (including the liquid from the can of tomatoes), bring to a boil, cover tightly, and simmer for 2 hours. Eat hot.

Note: If you don't have beef broth on hand, try chicken broth or 3 cups of water with 3 bouillon cubes.

Soybean Chili

Sometimes the familiar is really overlooked as food. For example, I was raised on a family farm and we harvested tons and tons of soybeans, but we never ate them. For some reason, we simply did not cook them. It never occurred to us to eat them, although we knew they were edible and used in soy sauce, tofu, cooking oil, and artificial hamburger patties. When I ran across a recipe for soybean chili, I wanted to try it but couldn't find soybeans on the market in my part of the country. I waited until harvest time, then hulled a few from the stalk. I now get a quart or two every year and save them for deer season.

> 1 pound ground venison
> 1 cup soybeans
> 1 can tomatoes (16-ounce size)
> 1 medium onion, chopped
> ¼ cup peanut oil
> 1 tablespoon chili powder
> salt and pepper to taste

In the morning, put the soybeans into a black pot and add 3 or 4 cups of water. Bring to a boil, reduce heat, cover, and simmer all day. (If you need the chili for lunch, soak the beans overnight in cold water, then cook them in the morning until tender.) When you are ready to proceed, brown the venison and the onion in the oil in a skillet. Chop the tomatoes and stir them and the liquid from the can in with the onions. Add salt, pepper, and chili powder. Combine the contents of the skillet and pot, mix well, and simmer for 20 or 30 minutes. Serve with crackers and watermelon rind preserves or sweet, crisp pickled cucumber rounds.

Venison with Quinoa

Here's a dish made with a grain from the Andes, cultivated by the Incas and other pre-Columbian Indians of that area. Quinoa is good stuff and is often cooked and eaten somewhat like rice in addition to being used in breadstuffs. This recipe is usually cooked with pork these days, but the Incas had no pork until the Spanish brought 'em some pigs. To be honest, I can't claim that the Incas made the dish with venison, either. They probably used more guinea pigs or llamas, as they did not have much good horned venison. But the quinoa and most of the other ingredients, including potatoes, peanuts, tomatoes, and peppers, are Andean. Here's what you'll need for my version.

1 pound cubed venison
½ pound venison sausage, sliced into ¼-inch wheels
½ pound quinoa
1 medium onion, chopped
2 medium potatoes, diced (see below)
2 cloves garlic, minced
1 large tomato, chopped
2 ounces roasted peanuts, ground (also see below)
2 cups milk
2 quarts water
¼ cup peanut oil
1 teaspoon red pepper flakes
salt
fresh parsley (for garnish)

Wash the quinoa and put it and the diced venison and sausage wheels into a pot with 2 quarts of water. Add the red pepper and salt. Bring to a boil, cover tightly, reduce heat, and simmer for 2 hours.

After about 1½ hours, heat the oil in a skillet. Sauté onions and garlic for a few minutes. Add peanuts and milk. Bring almost to a boil, then quickly reduce heat and simmer for 5 minutes.

Mix the contents of the skillet into the pot with the meat and quinoa. Add the diced potatoes and chopped tomato. Simmer until the potatoes are tender. Serve in bowls and garnish with chopped fresh parsley.

Variation: If you don't have any peanuts handy, use crunchy peanut butter. The recipe calls for two medium potatoes, diced, but it is even better with about 2 pounds of tiny new potatoes, cooked whole. I have also used 2 pounds of canned potatoes, which are usually small and require little cooking.

Venison and Green Tomatoes

When toying with the idea of using this recipe in this book, I happened to catch a short feature on television about the way tomatoes are raised south of Lake Okeechobee, Florida, picked green, and shipped to markets in the North. The commentator, an international food expert, failed to point out that such tomatoes have no taste, as compared with those that ripen on the vine. These latter are often called home-grown tomatoes, meaning vine-ripened tomatoes grown in the home garden or at least grown in the market area.

The green tomatoes are very tasty, however, if they are cooked while still green. They are not often available in most markets, but this may change now that the movie *Fried Green Tomatoes* has let the secret out. Remember that they can be cooked in other ways, as shown below. If green tomatoes aren't available, try this recipe with the delicious green husk, tomatoes, or *tomatillos*. These are popular in Mexico and are sometimes available north of the border. If you garden at home and have green tomatoes in summer, freeze some venison and try this recipe.

> 4 pounds venison
> milk
> ¼ cup cooking oil or fat
> 4 large green tomatoes, diced
> 4 medium potatoes, diced
> 4 medium onions, diced
> 4 stalks of celery, diced

Cut the venison into large chunks. Put these into a glass container and cover with milk. Marinate overnight. When ready to cook, drain the venison and brown it in hot oil in a stove-top Dutch oven or suitable pot. (If you prefer, brown the venison in a skillet and transfer it to a pot, without the pan drippings.) Barely cover the venison with water, bring to a boil, reduce heat, cover, and simmer for 2 hours or until tender. Add a little water if needed. Add the vegetables, salt, and pepper. Bring to a boil, reduce heat, cover, and simmer for 30 minutes, or until the vegetables are tender.

Venison and Green Peppers

Many people call this dish pepper steak, but to me, pepper steak (or steak *au poivre*) is grilled or broiled and has lots of black pepper worked into the surface. The recipe below is distinguished by bell peppers, soy sauce, and fresh ginger root. In other words, it's Oriental. I prefer to cook it in a wok, but a heavy skillet will do just fine.

> 1 pound venison steak
> 2 green peppers
> 1 medium onion
> fresh ginger root
> ¼ cup peanut oil
> ¼ cup soy sauce
> ¼ cup sake
> 3 teaspoons cornstarch

Cut the steak into thin strips no more than ¼ inch thick. (Slicing is easier if the meat is chilled or partly frozen.) Mix the soy sauce, sake, and cornstarch in a non-metallic bowl. Stir in the strips of steak and marinate for several hours. Stir every hour or so.

When you are ready to cook, core the green peppers and cut them lengthwise into canoe-shaped strips about 1 inch wide in the middle. Peel the onion, quarter it lengthwise, and separate the layers. Cut four ¼-inch-thick slices from the ginger root. Heat the oil in a wok or skillet and add the ginger, green pepper, and onion. Stir-fry for several minutes until tender. If you are using a skillet or a slick-surfaced wok, remove the peppers with a slotted spoon and drain on a brown bag. If you are using a wok with hammered sides and the right slope, drag the peppers and onions up the side, out of the oil. Drain the meat but reserve the marinade. Stir-fry the meat on high heat for about 2 minutes, adding a little of the marinade as you go. Add the peppers to the meat and stir-fry for another 2 minutes. Fish out the ginger and throw it away. Serve with steamed rice. If you are eating with knives and forks, use long-grained rice; with chopsticks, cook short-grained rice, which is sticky. (By the way, the strips of venison, along with the strips of green pepper, make this dish fairly easy to eat with chop-sticks as compared to garden peas and mashed potatoes.)

Variation: If you've got good fresh mushrooms, add them to the peppers and onions.

Stuffed Peppers

This recipe can be made by boiling some venison and chopping it, but I usually make it from leftover roast.

> 2 cups of cooked venison, diced
> 2 strips bacon
> 4 large green bell peppers
> 1 jalapeño, minced
> 1 medium onion, diced
> 1 tablespoon catsup
> salt and pepper

Preheat the oven to 350 degrees. Cut the tops off the bell peppers and take out the seeds and core. Fry the bacon in a skillet until crisp, then remove. Sauté the venison for a minute, then crumble the bacon and add it to the skillet along with the onion, jalapeño, catsup, salt, and pepper. (Some jalapeño peppers are very hot, so it's best to remove the seeds before mincing. Then wash your hands.) Mix everything and stuff the peppers. Stand the stuffed peppers in a pan and bake for about 45 minutes. Usually, one person will eat two peppers.

Note: Most cookbooks recommend that bell peppers be cored and boiled for a few minutes before they are stuffed. I don't think this step is necessary, but suit yourself. Most stuffed pepper recipes are too bland for me, so I add the jalapeño.

Corned Venison and Cabbage

Since the meat for this dish is soaked in a liquid, some Americans have connected the word *corned* with corn whiskey. Actually, the term has nothing to do with corn as we Americans know it. In the British Isles, the word *corn* was once applied to any grain, and the word goes back to the Anglo-Saxons whereas American corn (maize) wasn't known in Europe until it was brought in from America. In short, the word *corn* applied to wheat berries, oats, and other groats, all of which are smaller than the American maize kernels. By extension, the term was applied to salt crystals of about the same size. These crystals, often from sea salt, were mixed with water to form a brine. The meat went into the brine for a week or so, and was thus considered to be "corned."

Sea salt contains minerals, such as saltpeter (potassium nitrate), that help preserve meat and give it a reddish color. Table salt lacks these minerals, so they have been added back to corning solutions in an effort to preserve the corned beef. Spices and flavorings are also added. I like to go back to basics for my corned venison and use spring water or distilled water with wonderful sea salt (or kosher salt) in crystals about the size of a small wheat kernel. Try it.

2 or more venison roasts
1 gallon water
1 cup sea salt
½ cup brown sugar

Bring the water to a boil and dissolve the sea salt and brown sugar. Let it cool and put it into a crock or glass container of suitable size. (For a single small roast, I use a crockpot and mix only ½ gallon of water and ½ cup of sea salt.) Trim any fat off the roast and submerge it in the solution. Put a plate or saucer on it and then weight it down with another saucer or two. In other words, the meat should not be in contact with the air. Cover the container with a cloth and keep it in a cool place for two or three days. Rinse the meat well before cooking. Note that the recipe does not include the spices that are often added to corned meat these days. You can add them when you cook the corned meat. When you're ready, proceed with this old Irish recipe.

4 pounds corned venison
1 large cabbage or 2 medium cabbages
3 or 4 onions, golf ball size
1 large carrot, sliced
1 teaspoon powdered mustard
6 cloves
2 bay leaves
1 tablespoon chopped thyme
black pepper

Rinse the corned venison, fit it into a pot, and almost cover it with water. Add the carrots, then peel the onions and add them to the pot. Add the mustard, cloves, bay leaves, and pepper. Bring to a boil, cover, reduce heat, and simmer for 4 hours. Cut the cabbage into quarters and add to the top of the pot so that it steams. Cover and simmer for about 30 minutes, or until the cabbage is tender. Remove the cabbage and then the meat. (Save the broth for stock or soup.) Put the meat onto a platter and surround it with cabbage wedges. Serve hot.

I love this dish for a complete meal, served along with good bread. I like it especially with fried cornbread made with fine, white water-ground style cornmeal. If you want more formal fare, suitable for a Christmas dinner or other family gathering, try the New England boiled dinner below.

Note: If you want to corn venison for longer storage, use a preserver such as sodium nitrate or saltpeter. See the text starting on page 140.

New England Boiled Dinner

This wonderful dish, a full meal, goes back to Colonial days. I say it calls for corned venison, although it is usually cooked with corned beef brisket these days. It can contain a number of good American root vegetables, such as Jerusalem artichokes and wild potatoes, but I always want some cabbage, too. Sliced red beets are often served with this dish, but they should be cooked separately, peeled, and sliced.

I consider this dish to be fit for festive occasions, and I like it served up on a large platter, with the corned venison in the center and the vegetables piled around it.

> 5 or 6 pounds corned venison
> spices (to taste)
> ½ pound salt pork
> 1 large head cabbage
> 4 medium potatoes (or 12 small ones)
> 4 large carrots
> 3 parsnips (optional)
> 12 small onions (golf ball size)
> 3 medium turnip roots or rutabagas
> 8 medium beets (cooked separately)
> pepper

Put the corned venison into a large pot and cover it with water. (If your venison was not spiced during the corning process, add 1 tablespoon of pickling spice or a few cloves and three bay leaves.) Dice the salt pork and add it to the pot. Bring to a boil, reduce heat, cover, and simmer for 2 hours or until the venison is tender. Remove the venison and add all the vegetables except the cabbage and beets. They should be peeled and either diced or quartered. (I really prefer to use small whole vegetables, such as new potatoes, onions about the size of golf balls, and miniature carrots. If you use these, it's easy enough to adjust the numbers required since the measures don't have to be exact. Wild foods enthusiasts will want to try various edible tubers in this recipe.) Anyhow, bring the vegetables to a boil, add salt and pepper to taste (not much salt will be required), reduce heat, cover, and simmer for 15 minutes. Cut the cabbage into six or eight wedges; allow at least one wedge for each person. Bring to a new boil, reduce heat, cover, and simmer for 15 minutes. Return the venison to the pot and simmer for 10 minutes. Serve immediately with the venison in the center of a large platter surrounded by the boiled vegetables. And don't forget the boiled and sliced beets. They add color as well as flavor. Canned beets will do. Serve with plenty of good, hot bread.

Venison Cabbage Rolls

My sister introduced me to this dish some time ago, and it has become one of my favorites.

> 1 pound ground venison
> large cabbage leaves (at least 10)
> ¼ cup long-grain rice, uncooked
> 1 chicken egg
> 1 medium onion, chopped
> 1 can tomatoes (16-ounce size)
> 1 small can tomato paste (6-ounce size)
> butter or margarine
> salt and pepper to taste

Thoroughly mix the venison, rice, egg, tomato paste, onion, salt, and pepper. Boil or steam the cabbage leaves until tender. (A bamboo steamer is ideal, but an ordinary pot can be used.) Spoon some of the meat onto each cabbage leaf, roll it up, and fasten with a round toothpick. Heat a little butter or margarine in a large skillet and sauté the cabbage rolls for a few minutes. Chop the tomatoes and pour over the rolls along with the liquid from the can. Cover tightly and simmer for 1 hour.

These rolls can be served as a main dish with vegetables and bread or used along with another meat course.

EIGHT

Fried Venison and Skillet Specialties

There's something special about cooking in a cast-iron skillet or on a hand-held griddle. Perhaps that old black magic comes from a more direct contact with the food, especially when the skillet can be shaken back and forth instead of stirring the contents. Further, meat fried in a little oil in a skillet is different from that cooked in a deep fryer. For one thing, the meat in a skillet stays directly in touch with the bottom instead of floating in oil. The result can be a two-toned crunchy texture. This effect is especially desirable in fried chicken and is not entirely lost on venison. Also, a skillet requires only a modest amount of oil for frying, whereas most deep fryers need a gallon, even at today's prices. Still, a good deep fryer is the only way to go if you are frying food for a crowd. I like the free-standing deep fryers, fueled by rechargeable gas cylinders or by natural gas, that are being used more and more on the patio and in camp.

I'm a cast-iron skillet man, but pans of heavy-duty aluminum and ceramic-coated metal will also do a good job and are easier to keep in good shape. (Cast iron must be seasoned to prevent sticking and must always be treated with tender loving care.) Still, there are several advantages to cast iron. For one, it can be heated to a very high temperature without damaging or warping the material. This feature is essential for truly blackening fish and other meats, including venison. Another advantage for me is that I often start cooking on top of the stove and end up putting the skillet into the oven or under the broiler. This procedure isn't advisable with skillets having wooden or plastic handles, but most cast-iron skillets are sand-cast in one piece.

The complete skillet chef ought to have several pieces, prefer-ably of various sizes. I require three sizes: 8, 10¾, and 13 inches. The largest should have a lid (also available in cast iron) that fits tightly for cooking one-dish dinners for five or six people. I also like the new oval griddles, which are perfect for blackening food, cooking for one person, or making venison burgers for two.

Some of the recipes in this chapter are for skillets that will safely hold an inch or so of oil. Others can be cooked on griddles and still others are best cooked in a deep fryer. Some other skillet recipes are set forth in other chapters.

Fried Venison Cubes

This recipe works with almost any tender cut of venison. Very tough meat, however, should be simmered for a long while in a stew. Medium-tough meat can be cubed and sprinkled with commercial tenderizer following the directions on the package.

> 2 pounds venison
> peanut oil for deep frying
> ½ cup soy sauce
> ½ cup prepared mustard
> 1 medium onion, minced
> 2 cloves garlic, minced or crushed
> 1 teaspoon salt
> ¼ teaspoon cayenne pepper
> flour

Trim the fat and sinew from the venison and cut it into cubes of about 1 inch. Put the meat into a glass bowl or a plastic zip bag and add the soy sauce, mustard, onion, garlic, salt, and cayenne pepper. Marinate for 2 hours or longer. When you are ready to cook, rig for deep frying, heating the peanut oil to 375 degrees. Drain the meat and dredge it in flour, coating all sides. Quickly fry about ½ pound. This should take only 4 minutes, unless you have cut your venison into larger pieces. When done, the outside should be crisp and brown, and the inside pink. When the first batch is done, take it out with a slotted spoon and drain it on a brown bag. Fry the next batch of about ½ pound. The idea is to fry small amounts at a time so that the oil doesn't cool too much. If you are using a large deep fryer containing a gallon or so of oil, you can, of course, cook the whole batch at once.

Skillet Venison

Several cuts of venison can be used to prepare this dish. I prefer strips about ½ inch thick and 3 inches long, cut across the grain. I have also used tenderloin strips cut with the grain, but I prefer meat of short fiber because cutting with the grain makes the pieces stringy. Try strips cut from venison round steaks.

> 2 pounds venison strips
> ¼ cup bacon drippings or cooking oil
> 1 cup V-8 juice
> ¼ cup red wine
> 8 ounces fresh mushrooms, sliced
> 1 medium onion, diced
> salt and pepper
> rice (cooked separately)

Sauté the mushrooms and onions in the bacon drippings or oil for a few minutes in a large, heavy skillet. Remove with a slotted spoon. Increase the heat and brown the venison strips. Add the V-8 juice, wine, vegetables, and salt and pepper to taste. Bring to a light boil, reduce heat, cover tightly, and simmer for 1 hour. Stir once or twice and add a little water if needed. Serve over rice.

This recipe is a good one for use in a deer camp, where bacon drippings from breakfast can be used. V-8 juice always comes in handy in camp and is available in cans of several sizes. Also, be sure to try this recipe with wild onions or ramps, including a few chopped green tops. These are almost always stronger than garden onions, but they have a wonderful flavor, especially in a skillet dish. If you don't have wine in camp, try a touch of vinegar or merely add a little water.

107

Venison au Jus

The term *au jus* applies to meat cooked, usually on low heat for a long time, in its own juices. I've cooked venison au jus a number of times, but since venison is a rather dry meat, I always use a little liquid. Actually, I seldom use an exact recipe for venison au jus, but for this book I have written down the ingredients and measures from a recent batch. I highly recommend it.

> 2 pounds thinly sliced venison
> 2 strips bacon
> 1 medium onion, chopped
> 4 ounces mushrooms, sliced
> ¼ cup red wine vinegar
> 2 tablespoons Worcestershire sauce
> salt and pepper to taste

Fry the bacon in a skillet. Remove it and crumble the strips. Brown the meat, onions, and mushrooms in the bacon drippings. Add the red wine vinegar, crumbled bacon, Worcestershire sauce, salt, and pepper. Reduce heat and simmer uncovered for 30 or 40 minutes, stirring from time to time. Add a little water or beef stock if necessary. Serve with rice and mixed stir-fried vegetables.

This dish can be cooked with slices of tenderloin, backstrap, or other good cuts of venison. It works best when the slices are about ¼ inch thick.

Blackened Venison

A cast-iron griddle or skillet is required for this dish. A Dutch oven is really too large, since the sides become heat sinks and also get in the way. A lid from a camp-style Dutch oven will do nicely, however. Also, a hot fire is required in order to heat the griddle. Charcoal doesn't burn very hot and won't do. Use wood coals or gas heat.

Actually, because of the smoke, this dish should not be cooked indoors unless you've got a fireplace with a good draw. The problem is in getting rid of the smoke. Also, the technique described here won't work with some "blackening" methods set forth in other publications, such as putting butter on the griddle "to keep the meat from sticking." If your griddle is hot enough for blackening, it will burn up butter immediately, making even more smoke, and will give the meat an undesirable flavor. If you want to proceed, here's what you'll need.

> venison steaks, sliced ⅜ inch thick
> spice mix (see below)
> melted butter

Build your fire and let the coals burn down. Mix all the spices (see below). When you are ready to cook, flip-flop each steak in melted butter, coat each side heavily with the spice mixture, and lay on the hot griddle. Use good no-slip tongs for this, not a fork. Sizzle for 1 minute, then turn it over and sizzle the other side. Put the steak on a serving platter, top with a spoonful of melted butter, and spread it over the spices, which should have formed a crusty surface over the meat. Serve hot with plenty of cooling green salad, tall drinks, and bread.

The spice mix can be varied for this recipe, but don't cut back very much on the paprika. It is a mild spice (made from dried and ground bell peppers) and serves as a sort of filler for the mix. A thick coating is necessary for the dish to be at its best, and this prevents the meat from sticking to the hot griddle. The same technique can be used with fish fillets (about ½ inch thick) and boned chicken or pheasant breast pounded flat. Even flattened duck breast works. Commercial spice mixes are available for various meats; here's the recipe I use for venison and other red meats.

> 1 tablespoon black pepper
> 2 tablespoons paprika
> 2 teaspoons cayenne pepper
> 1 tablespoon sea salt
> 5 teaspoons mustard seeds
> 5 teaspoons fennel seeds

With a mortar and pestle, crush the sea salt, mustard seeds, and fennel seeds, then mix all the spices in a pint jar with a lid and store in a dark, cool place until you are ready to cook.

I like to prepare blackened venison on a campfire with spices mixed at home. A cast-iron skillet is a bit heavy for backpacking, but some new oval griddles are just right for blackening a steak or frying two eggs. Also remember that you don't have to have a cooking utensil for this dish. Just rake a mound of red-hot coals from the fire and put the steak right on top of it for ½ minute. Then turn and sizzle the other side. You can also cook this recipe on a glowing back log from your fire. Typically, it's a rather large green log used to bank smaller pieces of wood. When the back log starts to burn, roll it away from the fire a quarter of a turn and lay the steaks onto the hot spot. Cooking in this manner is a lot of fun and could come in handy one day as a survival technique.

No-Fat Griddle Steaks

Anyone really serious about no-fat cooking but who doesn't care for all the spices used in the blackening ought to try this method. First, cut the steaks on the thick side, about 2 inches. Then heat a cast-iron griddle quite hot (but short of the blackening extremes) and sprinkle a little salt onto the cooking surface. That's right. Salt. No grease. Not even spray. Then, using tongs, put the steak onto the griddle and sear for ½ minute or so, then turn and sear the other side. Reduce the heat and cook until the steaks are medium-rare, or to your taste. A good deal depends on the heat and the thickness of the meat, so cutting into a piece to check for doneness is the only reliable test. After cooking by this method a time or two, you can learn to test the doneness by looking at the sides of the steaks.

Most practitioners of this method recommend that each steak be topped with a chunk of butter, sprinkled with a little pepper, and served on a warmed plate. I agree, especially with venison steaks, but the meat is surprisingly moist if cooked quickly and not too done. (Of course, it is also lower in fat if you don't add the butter.) When using this method, I prefer to use a coarse sea salt or kosher salt, which I say has more flavor than regular table salt. Rock salt is little too coarse, however, unless you crush it into smaller pieces.

Venison Steak au Poivre

This French method of preparing a steak works to advantage with venison if you have tender meat. It's best to avoid steaks cut from the leg and use meat from either the loin or the tenderloin. I prefer to make chops from the loin, cutting them 1 inch thick, or to butterfly 2-inch sections of the tenderloin, ending up with a piece 1 inch thick.

> 2 pounds tender venison steaks
> 2 tablespoons butter
> salt and freshly crushed pepper (rather coarse)
> 2 ounces good whiskey

Crush some peppercorns with your mortar and pestle or buy coarse pepper at the supermarket. Sprinkle your steaks lightly with salt and then press a liberal amount of pepper into both sides of the meat. Melt the butter in a skillet and heat it almost to the smoking point. Sear the steaks on both sides, then sauté until the meat is rare or medium-rare. Quickly put the steaks onto a heated serving platter. Use your spatula or wooden spoon to dislodge any bits of meat that may have stuck to the bottom of the pan. Pour the whiskey into the pan and shake it around for several minutes. Pour the sauce over the meat and serve.

Variation: Brandy may be used instead of whiskey. Add ¼ cup of minced green onions (including part of the green tops) and ½ cup of thick beef stock. Stir and simmer until the liquid is reduced by half. Then pour it over the steaks and serve. If you use this method, be sure to keep the steaks warm while waiting. Cold venison simply won't do.

Carpet Bag Steak

The Australians invented a recipe for combining the oyster and the beefsteak. It can be used with other tender cuts of meat, such as backstrap of venison or kangaroo. Since venison backstrap is smaller than most beefsteaks, I recommend the use of small oysters. For the best flavor, the oysters ought to be right from the shell and *not* washed in fresh water.

111

boneless venison chops or tender cutlets, thick
small oysters
melted butter
salt and pepper
parsley, chopped

With a sharp filleting knife, cut a pocket into each venison chop, working from the side. The chop should be 1½ inches thick. Work a little salt and pepper inside the pocket, then insert an oyster. The pocket should be large enough, or the oyster small enough, to permit the slit to be completely closed. Skewer shut with a couple of round toothpicks inserted at such an angle that the steaks lie flat. Prepare as many of these chops or cutlets as you need to feed everybody.

In a skillet, heat a little butter and cook the chops for 4 or 5 minutes on each side, turning once. Put them onto a heated serving platter and sprinkle with parsley, salt, and pepper. Scrape the pan with a wooden spatula and pour the drippings over the steaks. Eat immediately.

Note: In one of his books, James Beard suggested putting a small ice cube inside hamburger patties before they are grilled or broiled, saying that the ice will melt and keep the inside moist. It's a great idea for ground venison, which tends to be dry, and I suggest that an oyster has almost as much moisture as an ice cube and a lot more personality and flavor.

Country and Smother-Fried Steaks

Recipes for these steaks are covered elsewhere, but a recap may be in order here. I say a country steak is about ½ inch thick, beaten with a meat mallet or the edge of a plate, sprinkled with salt and pepper, well dusted with flour, and fried with a little hot grease in a skillet. When the steaks are done, part of the grease is poured out and a little flour is stirred in. The flour is cooked for a few minutes, then water or coffee is slowly added, stirring as you go, until it becomes gravy. It is served over rice, mashed potatoes, or biscuits.

With smother-fried steaks, the meat is browned and then

cooked in the gravy for an hour or so, or until the meat is fork tender. Both methods are very good, if properly done. Obviously, country-fried steak works best with tender meat and the smother-fried steak with tough meat. Of course, there are variations, but I always like lots of freshly ground black pepper in my gravy. Also see my wife's recipe for breakfast steaks in chapter 12.

Chinese Tenderloin

Tenderloin of venison is delicate, and cooking it very long robs it of flavor and toughens it. One of my favorite recipes for it comes from Chinese cuisine, in which meat is sometimes simmered in a thin sauce and then fried for a minute or two. I love the flavor and often cook quail, fryer rabbits, and young squirrels by this method.

> tenderloin
> peanut oil
> 1 can of chicken broth (10½-ounce size)
> 1 cup soy sauce
> ½ cup rice wine or sherry
> 4 slices fresh ginger root
> black pepper

Get your deep fryer ready and start heating the peanut oil, aiming for a high temperature of 375 degrees. Cut the tenderloin into serving size pieces. Mix the chicken broth, soy sauce, rice wine or sherry, pepper, and ginger in a saucepan. (A slice of ginger is about ¼ inch thick, made from a root of about 1 inch in diameter.) Bring the sauce to a boil, reduce heat, and let it set for a while to absorb the ginger flavor. Increase the heat and simmer the meat for 5 or 6 minutes.

By now the oil should be ready for frying. Remove the tenderloin pieces from the sauce and dry them quickly with paper towels—but do not allow them to cool very much. Put the tenderloin into the hot oil and fry for 3 minutes. Do not overcook.

Save the stock from this recipe. You can use it several times if you refrigerate it.

NINE

Grilling, Broiling, and Barbecuing Venison

Before getting into a number of recipes that can be used for cooking up good kabobs and similar dishes, I would like to discuss two very similar methods of cooking meats. Both make use of direct radiant heat, usually quite close to the meat. In grilling, the meat is placed above the heat, usually on a grid, spit, or skewer. This method also puts the meat above the smoke and the vapors caused by the fire, either from the burning of wood or from heating the drippings from the meat. The smoke imparts flavor to the meat and many people add wood chips to a charcoal or gas fire to increase the amount and quality of the smoke. Although I don't object to a little smoke, I don't think it complements the flavor of venison or beef as much as it does pork, bear, and chicken. But that's just one man's opinion. Also, I must point out that grilling can quickly ruin a good piece of venison, which becomes dry and tough when well done. Anyone who likes meat well done would be advised to cook it by steaming or boiling, not by grilling.

Broiling is much like grilling, except that the meat is under the fire instead of over it. This arrangement all but eliminates the smoke effect. Broiled venison can be tasty, but as with grilling, the dry heat can quickly ruin a good piece of meat. This method is not recommended for people who like their meat well done. The term "broiling" is also used in some cookbooks and in the restaurant business to denote meat that is cooked either on a grill (as in charbroiling) or a griddle (pan broiling).

In any case, the next recipe is ideal for people who aren't quite sure how to cook venison on a grill; the bacon helps keep the meat moist. Also, it's hard to go wrong with most mushrooms on the grill. They are good at any stage of cooking, short of being burned.

Good Ol' Boy Kabobs

Several friends of mine, all good ol' boys, grill venison kabobs pretty much by the recipe below. Most of them proceed with a beer in one hand and a bottle of lemon-pepper seasoning salt in the other. (Variations abound, and, of course, some prefer celery salt or garlic salt.) In addition to helping prevent the meat from drying out over direct heat, the smoked bacon adds considerably to the flavor of the kabobs.

> tender venison chunks
> smoked bacon
> lemon-pepper seasoning salt
> whole mushrooms the size of golf balls

Build a charcoal or wood coal fire. Trim the venison, cut it into 1½-inch chunks, and sprinkle with lemon-pepper seasoning. Wrap a piece of venison with half a strip of bacon and thread it onto a skewer, arranging it so that the ends of the bacon face in. Next, skewer a mushroom and push it down next to the ends of bacon. Add another piece of bacon-wrapped venison, another mushroom, and so on until the skewer is as full as you want it. Prepare a skewer for each person. Grill close to coals for several minutes, or until the bacon begins to brown. Turn and sprinkle lightly with lemon-pepper seasoning. Cook the other side until bacon starts to turn brown. When the bacon looks ready, take the kabob off the grill.

Variation: Many good ol' boys want to marinate the venison before cooking it, which I allow and encourage if the meat is not perfect. I like ordinary cow's milk for a marinade, but many of my buddies prefer Dale's steak seasoning, which is merely sprinkled on the meat. If you can't find Dale's, try a mixture of half soy sauce and half Worcestershire sauce, or teriyaki sauce.

Alaskan Kabobs

According to *Alaska Magazine's Cabin Cookbook*, kabobs of venison are sometimes marinated in a mixture of juice from the lowbush cranberry along with a few spices. Red wine vinegar can be used instead of the juice. I have also cooked it with unsweetened juice from regular cranberries, which I zapped in a food processor, and found it to be quite tasty.

tender venison, cut into 1-inch cubes
¼ cup lowbush cranberry juice
¼ cup oil
¼ teaspoon garlic salt
¼ teaspoon onion salt
¼ teaspoon celery salt
¼ teaspoon cracked black pepper
onions, mushrooms, green peppers

Mix oil, juice, and spices, then marinate the venison overnight, or for several hours. When you are ready to cook, build a good fire and burn it down to hot coals. Thread the meat onto skewers, alternating with chunks of onion, pieces of green pepper, and mushrooms. Grill the kabobs close to the hot coals for several minutes, until done to your liking. Baste a couple of times with the leftover marinade.

Hawaiian Venison Kabobs

Fresh pineapple, quartered and grilled over charcoal, is a great treat. It is also good when cooked with kabobs, and works nicely with teriyaki marinades. Pineapple also tenderizes meat.

2 pounds tender venison cut into 1-inch chunks
1 fresh pineapple, cut into 1-inch chunks
juice of 1 lemon
2 cloves garlic, minced
¼ cup soy sauce
¼ cup dark brown sugar
¼ cup sunflower oil
½ teaspoon freshly grated ginger
salt and pepper to taste

116

Mix lemon juice, garlic, soy sauce, brown sugar, sunflower oil, and grated ginger. Put the venison into a glass bowl, cover it with the marinade, and refrigerate for 6 to 8 hours. When you are ready to cook, build a charcoal fire. Drain the venison, but save the marinade. Salt and pepper each chunk of venison and string them onto skewers, alternating with pineapple chunks. Grill close to the heat for about 4 minutes on each side, or until the meat is medium-rare. Baste once or twice with the leftover marinade. Do not overcook. Feeds four to six.

Note: This recipe can be used on a stove-top grill or under a broiler. The main requirement is to cook the meat quickly without getting it too done.

Easy Kabobs, Easy Steaks

More and more people are marinating venison with zesty Italian salad dressing these days, and I highly recommend the practice. The dressing has oil, vinegar, and spices, all of which complement the flavor of grilled and broiled venison. To proceed, put the venison into a glass bowl and sprinkle a little of the dressing over it. Toss the meat to coat all sides and marinate for ½ hour or longer. Then cook it on a grill or under a broiler, either as kabobs or steaks. Also try strips of marinated steak rolled up with a piece of thin bacon, making a wheel. Pin the wheel with round toothpicks and broil or grill. When the meat is almost done, salt and pepper it to taste. Eat hot.

Grilled Venison Steaks with Garlic

This recipe works for a charcoal grill and indoor stove-top grills as well as for broiling, which I use more than the other methods. It works best with tender meat about 1 inch thick.

> steaks for two
> 1 clove garlic
> ½ cup olive oil
> salt and pepper

If you are feeding more than two people, increase the olive oil and garlic. About 2 hours before cooking, slice the garlic in half lengthwise and rub all sides of the steak, pressing down on the garlic as you go. Put the steaks and garlic halves in a bowl and pour the olive oil over them, stirring to coat all sides of the meat. Marinate for about 2 hours.

When you are ready to cook, build a hot charcoal fire or heat up the gas grill. Cook the meat close to the heat for about 4 minutes on each side. Do not overcook. If you don't have a lot of experience at the grill, cut into a piece of the meat to test for doneness before serving. Season to taste during the last few minutes of cooking.

BARBECUE AS A NOUN

Not long ago, a friend of mine, a lawyer, called me about a line of custom bass lures that I once made and marketed. I told him that I had quit the business and was now writing about fish and game cooking, and that I was always on the lookout for good ideas and recipes. He said that, oh yes, he had been hunting in Wyoming and their guide barbecued an elk steak that was out of this world. I asked for the particulars, and he said that the fellow had barbecued it on a grill over wood coals. When questioned about the sauce, he said that a sauce wasn't used. Instead, the meat had been marinated in Dale's steak seasoning. So, what the people ate was simply a grilled elk steak, I say, and had very little in common with what I call barbecue.

Not long ago, I told a book editor in Maine about the elk "barbecue," and he said that some people in that neck of the woods didn't realize that the word could be a noun as well as a verb. Indeed, it can. As a noun, it means cooked meat with lots of thick sauce on it. The meat can be cooked by grilling, broiling, steaming, baking, or other methods. Some people even make "barbecue" in a microwave oven. Almost always it is best to apply the sauce to the meat during the last 5 minutes of the cooking process. Be warned that a thick sauce with a tomato base (or with sugar in it) should not be used as a baste during the entire grilling or broiling process. It will burn and disflavor your good meat.

Further, I say barbecue sauce is best when used on pork or bear, but it can also be used on venison. The recipes that follow are my best recommendations.

Big Foot Venison Barbecue

Here's a recipe that I cook with the aid of a Big Foot Grill set up in my back yard and one or two crockpots (or stove-top Dutch ovens) set up in my kitchen. If you like the smell of good meat and hardwood smoke and enjoy tending a fire, try this method. But remember that it's an all-afternoon project. It's best to have a lawn chair near the grill—and plenty of beer.

I prefer to cook this on a fire made of hickory, pecan, or some other good wood. And I like green wood. Dry wood can be used, but it burns too fast to suit me. Charcoal will also do a good job, but it doesn't smell as good as wood and costs more. It's best to have the meat well above the hot coals. What I like about the Big Foot is that it's easy to adjust the height of the grill above the coals.

> 1 venison hindquarter
> 2 cups butter or margarine
> 1 cup freshly squeezed lemon juice
> 1 cup Worcestershire sauce
> salt and black pepper

I use a large chunk of meat for this recipe, usually a whole hindquarter, including the ham and the rump roast. In fact, the whole hind part of the deer can be used, which would include both hindquarters and the saddle. (This cut is called the baron.) Smaller cuts can also be used and the basting sauce can be adjusted as needed. Start by building a good hardwood fire and rigging the Big Foot nearby. (If you don't have a Big Foot, rig some sort of rack well above the fire. The advantages of the Big Foot are that it can be adjusted easily and it can be swung away from the fire if things get too hot, or when you are ready to slice the meat.) When the coals burn down a bit, put the meat onto the grill. Melt the butter in a pot, preferably of cast iron, and stir in the Worcestershire sauce and lemon juice. Remember that you've got to brush the sauce onto the meat from time to time. I find that a paintbrush works just fine for this purpose. A store-bought or homemade barbecue mop can also be used.

When the flame from the fire dies down a little, I swing the meat over the fire and start the cooking. I usually keep the meat well above the heat and may add some green wood around the edge of the fire to make smoke. You don't want a roaring fire at this point. Cook the meat for about 30 minutes and then turn it over. It's best to swing the meat away from the heat and turn the chunks by hand, with the aid of cooking gloves. A three-tine pitchfork with a short handle may help.

Baste the top of the meat, then sprinkle on a little salt and pepper. I use freshly ground pepper because it smells better. Cook for another 30 minutes or so and turn again. Baste. Sprinkle with salt and pepper. Continue this cooking and turning until your meat starts to brown. At this point, slice off the cooked part, getting chunks about 2 inches thick. These should be browned on the outside and juice red on the inside. Put these chunks into a large bowl and baste with the sauce. Turn the meat over, then take the partly cooked chunks into the house and put them into a crockpot. Turn the heat to high and cover. Get a beer and return to the Big Foot. Cut more chunks from the top and repeat the process. When the crockpot is about half full, reduce the heat to low. Keep going until all the meat has been cut from the bone or until the crockpot is full. Start another crockpot and keep going until you have most of the meat off the bones. The process will become much quicker toward the end. Save the bone for soup.

Keep the meat in the crockpot on low until you are ready to eat. Remember that the secret of this dish depend on two things: You want a slice of meat that is done on one side and medium-rare on the inside. It's best to adjust the depth of your cuts as you go, making sure that the inside of the meat is at least partly cooked and not dripping much blood. Second, you want lots of wood smoke.

Variation: In addition to the sauce above, use a thick tomato-based barbecue sauce of your choice. For best flavor, use the barbecue sauce sparingly and only after the chunk meat has been sliced off the ham. Putting tomato-based sauce over the fire is not recommended by me.

Easy Barbecued Venison Sandwiches

This skillet dish is easy to prepare, using a commercial barbecue sauce. You'll need tender meat. If you suspect that what you have on hand is tough, use a meat tenderizer. Trim off all fat and sinew with a sharp knife, ending up with cubes about ⅜ inch in diameter. The onion used in the recipe can be grated or minced.

> 2 pounds chopped venison
> fat or cooking oil
> 1 large onion, grated or minced
> 1 cup prepared barbecue sauce
> ¼ cup prepared mustard
> 2 tablespoons dark brown sugar
> 2 tablespoons vinegar
> salt and pepper to taste

In a large skillet, brown the meat quickly in a little oil or fat. I like to cover the bottom of the pan well with bacon drippings, but health food advocates will yell for vegetable oil sprayed from a can. Add the onions and stir. Then salt and pepper to taste and stir in the other ingredients. Increase the heat, bring to a simmer, reduce heat, cover tightly, and simmer for 30 minutes, stirring from time to time. Add a little salt or pepper if needed. Serve on large buns. Pickles and Boston baked beans served on the side go nicely with this sandwich, but potato chips or potato salad will do.

Easy Barbecued Venison Ribs

If you like to gnaw bones, as I do, and don't mind getting your fingers in a mess, this may be the recipe for you. Cut the ribs into serving-size pieces and simmer them in water along with a bay leaf or two until they are tender. Drain the ribs and dunk them in commercial barbecue sauce. Grill for 5 minutes over wood coals or charcoal, or broil in the oven. Turn and baste after 2 minutes. Serve hot, along with plenty of barbecue or garlic bread, Boston baked beans, and salad or cole slaw. If you want something a little hot and different, try basting the ribs during the last 5 minutes with Pickapepper sauce.

121

TEN

Venison Pies

The first true pies were made by the Romans with peacock, wild boar, and other good meats. The English improved on the idea, developing some of the more famous recipes, such as steak and kidney pie and blackbird pie. According to the *Progressive Farmer's Southern Cookbook*, "'Pye,' as it came to us from the English, featured a main dish of meat, game, and fowl baked in deep flaky crusts. The dessert pie as we know it today is essentially American."

In any case, the pie is a great way to cook venison. Here are some of my favorite recipes.

Venison and Blackbird Pie

Any small bird can be used in this recipe, and for centuries songbirds and sparrows have been eaten—and even marketed—in Europe. Before gathering American ingredients for this recipe, be warned that red-winged blackbirds and other species may be protected by law in some areas. On the other hand, some other blackbirds, or rice birds, can be taken legally and in very large numbers with no closed season. Often, shooting rice birds will help farmers—and these off-season birds may open up a whole new ball game for you.

This venison and blackbird recipe is one of my favorites. My mother cooked it for me years ago whenever the blackbirds or rice birds started flocking on our farm. Often a single shot from a 12-gauge would drop enough birds for a pie. I don't know the proper way to clean these birds, but I merely pull back the skin, lift the breast plate with my finger, and cut the wings off with kitchen shears. No knife is required.

The recipe below calls for 24 small blackbirds, or rice birds. If you've got larger birds, such as crows, skin them, fillet out each side of breast, and cut them into thumb-sized slices. If you don't have blackbirds or crows, try doves, snipe, or other small birds. If you don't hunt birds, buy a duck at the supermarket and cut the meat into bite-size pieces.

> 24 blackbirds, breasted
> 1 pound tender venison
> 8 slices of bacon
> 4 medium potatoes
> 4 medium carrots
> 10 green onions (with tops)
> 8 ounces fresh mushrooms
> flour
> water
> 1 cup sherry
> 3 hard-boiled chicken eggs
> pie pastry

Fry the bacon in a stove-top Dutch oven until crisp. Remove and drain it on paper towels. Cut the venison into small pieces about the size of the bird breasts. Salt and pepper the breasts and venison, then shake in a bag with flour. In the bacon drippings, stir-fry the bird breasts and venison pieces for 5 or 6 minutes on high heat. (Do not overcook.) Put the bacon back into the pot and add water until it reaches the top of the meat. Cover, reduce the heat, and simmer for 1 hour. While waiting, peel the potatoes and cut them into slices ¼ inch thick. Scrape the carrots and cut them into ¼-inch wheels. Peel the green onions and cut them into 1-inch lengths, along with about half of the tops. (If you don't have green onions, try medium onions diced and a few sprigs of green stuff, such as parsley.) Slice the mushrooms.

After the venison and bird breasts have simmered for 1 hour or so, mix in all the vegetables and sherry. Add enough water to almost cover the mixture. Bring to a boil, reduce heat, and cover. While waiting, preheat the oven to 400 degrees. After simmering the pot for 30 minutes, carefully slice the eggs and add to the pot in a layer. Cut the pastry into strips and crisscross the strips on top, leaving diamond-shaped holes. Bake the pie uncovered for 20 minutes, or until the pastry is browned. Delicious.

Variation: Use halves of refrigerated biscuits instead of pie pastry. Also remember that ready-made, frozen pie crusts can be purchased at the supermarket.

This pie can also be made in camp with an old-fashioned camp Dutch oven with a flanged lid designed for holding coals. Instead of browning the pastry in an oven, cover the pot with the flanged lid and pile red hot coals on top. (It helps to start with a preheated lid.) When the coals burn down, the pastry should be browned. If it isn't, stir the strips into the mixture—and call the recipe "venison and birds with dumplings."

Easy Venison Pie

Don't let the short list of ingredients for this dish fool you. It's very tasty. The meat can be from any good cut, including tenderloin or loin. Usually, I make it from "cutlets" sliced from a roast taken from the hind leg. If the slices are large, I cut them into pieces about 2 inches square. The thickness should be ½ inch.

2 pounds venison slices
3 or 4 medium to large potatoes
3 or 4 medium to large onions
3 or 4 strips of bacon
salt and pepper to taste

Preheat the oven to 250 degrees. Peel and cut the potatoes and onions into ½-inch slices. Grease the bottom and sides of a Pyrex baking dish (about 7 x 9 inches) with a strip of bacon. Put a layer of potatoes on the bottom of the dish. Add a layer of meat, then a layer of onions. Sprinkle on a little salt and pepper. Repeat the layers. Almost cover with water. Sprinkle on a little more salt and pepper. Cover with strips of bacon. Bake for 2 or 3 hours or until the meat is tender. If the bacon doesn't brown, turn on the broiler for a few minutes toward the end. I like the gravy from this dish served over rice.

Variations: This dish can be topped with a pie crust instead of bacon, in which case a little bacon grease, oil, or margarine should be brushed over each layer of meat and the bottom of the dish. Also, this dish makes a good choice for cooking in camp with a Dutch oven, for three reasons: It lends itself to slow cooking, it requires basic ingredients that are easy to carry, and it's a hearty one-dish meal, although biscuits or other bread will come in handy for sopping the gravy.

Old-Timey Venison Pie

Here's an old recipe, the sort of pie that was cooked in a Dutch oven beside the hearth. I like to make it in a cast-iron skillet or with another skillet that has an oven-proof handle. A skillet and an oven-proof casserole dish can be used instead. If your meat is tough, treat it with a commercial meat tenderizer before cooking.

> 2 pounds tender venison, cut into 1-inch cubes
> 2 cups potatoes, diced
> 1 large onion, diced
> ¼ cup flour
> ¼ cup vegetable oil
> salt and pepper to taste
> ½ teaspoon thyme, minced (or ¼ teaspoon dried)
> pie pastry
> 2 cups water

Preheat the oven to 450 degrees. Salt and pepper the meat and shake in a bag with the flour. Heat the oil in the skillet and brown the venison and onions. Add 2 cups of water and bring to a light boil. Add potatoes and thyme. Reduce heat, cover, and simmer for 2 hours. Stir from time to time and add a little water, if needed, and add salt and pepper to taste. Cut the pastry into strips about 1 inch wide and crisscross these atop the mixture, forming a lattice. Bake for 10 or 12 minutes, or until the crust is browned.

Variation: As stated above, I usually cook this dish in a skillet, which is put onto the table atop a cast-iron trivet. If you want to use a casserole dish, transfer the ingredients from the skillet to the dish, then top with the pie crust and bake for about 15 minutes, or until the crust is browned.

Venison Tamale Pie

This popular southwestern dish is a wonderful way to cook no-fat ground venison. It can be made with various kinds of chili peppers, whether fresh or canned. The canned chilies I have in mind are green ones in 4-ounce cans, coded according to hotness, instead of pickled jalapeños. Of course, any sort of hot pepper can be used.

Filling
1½ pounds ground venison
1 can stewed tomatoes (16-ounce size)
1 package frozen whole kernel corn (10-ounce size)
1 medium onion, chopped
1 bell pepper, chopped
1 can green chilies, mild (4-ounce size)
2 cloves garlic, minced
1 cup pitted black olives
½ cup grated cheddar cheese
½ cup vegetable oil
2 tablespoons cornmeal
1 tablespoon chili powder
1 teaspoon salt
½ teaspoon black pepper

Heat the oil in a large skillet with an oven-proof handle. (A 13-inch cast-iron skillet is ideal. A Dutch oven or even two smaller oven-proof skillets can be used.) Sauté the onion, garlic, and green pepper for a few minutes. Add the ground venison and brown. Add the tomatoes and juice, corn, olives, chili peppers, cornmeal, chili powder, cheddar cheese, salt, and pepper. Stir well. Simmer for 30 minutes. While waiting, preheat the oven to 400 degrees and prepare the topping, as directed below.

Topping
1 cup cornmeal
3 cups water
1 teaspoon salt

In a saucepan, boil the water and add the cornmeal and salt. Simmer and stir constantly until you have a thick mush. Pour the mush into the skillet over the pie filling and spread evenly. Bake for 30 minutes. Feeds four to six.

Venison and Kidney Pie

This old recipe, usually made with beefsteak and kidney, can also be made with venison and venison kidneys or with venison and lamb kidneys. The exact amount of kidney isn't critical, so use what you've got. The recipe is British, but it was also used extensively by the early American colonists.

2½ pounds tender venison
venison kidneys (1 or 2 sets)
cooking oil
flour
1 large onion, diced
8 ounces fresh mushrooms, sliced
¼ cup fresh parsley, chopped
½ cup beef stock
½ cup red wine
1 tablespoon Worcestershire sauce
salt and pepper
pastry for 9-inch pie crust

Cut the venison into 1-inch chunks. Trim the membrane from the kidneys, then cut them into 1-inch chunks. Sprinkle the cubed venison and kidneys with salt and pepper and shake in a bag with a little flour. In a stove-top Dutch oven, heat a little oil and brown the cubes, doing a few at a time and draining them on a brown bag. Add a little oil as needed. When all the meat is browned, sauté the onion, mushrooms, and parsley for 4 or 5 minutes on low heat. Pour off grease, if any, and add the beef stock, wine, Worcestershire sauce, salt, and pepper. Increase the heat, add the meat, and bring to a boil. Reduce heat, cover, and simmer for 2 hours.

Preheat the oven to 400 degrees and prepare a 9-inch pie crust or use store-bought pastry. Grease a round 2-quart casserole dish. Spoon in the filling, then top with the pastry. Cut slits into the pastry or punch it several times with a fork. Bake for 40 minutes or until the pie is bubbly and the crust is browned.

Variation: There are thousands of recipes for this pie, and one of the best contains fresh oysters as well as kidney and steak. Try a dozen small freshly shucked oysters mixed in with other ingredients, then cut back to ¼ cup wine and ¼ cup beef stock.

Easy Venison Quiche

This recipe calls for a single pie crust; I usually use one from the supermarket, frozen inside an aluminum pan. Your favorite home-made crust can also be used.

> ½ pound ground venison
> 2 strips bacon
> 1½ cups shredded cheddar cheese
> ½ cup milk
> ½ cup mayonnaise
> ½ cup chopped green onions (with part of tops)
> 2 medium chicken eggs
> 1 tablespoon cornstarch
> salt and pepper
> 9-inch unbaked pie crust

Preheat the oven to 350 degrees. Fry the bacon in a skillet until browned. Drain the bacon on absorbent paper. Brown the ground venison, along with the chopped green onions. (I use about half of the green onion tops.) Lightly whisk the eggs in a bowl along with the milk, mayonnaise, and cornstarch. Stir this mixture and the shredded cheddar into the browned venison, along with a little salt and pepper. Turn the mixture into the crust and bake for 30 to 40 minutes in the center of the oven until the pie is golden brown on top. The quiche is done when a kitchen knife inserted into the center comes out clean.

Mincemeat Pie

This pie is an old English dish dating back to the Middle Ages. According to *Larousse Gastronomique,* it is made without meat in England but in America it is made with beef or venison. I believe that the American version is a combination of the British mince pie and the native Indian pemmican, which contains ground venison, animal fat, and dried berries. (For more about pemmican, see chapter 11.) In any case, mincemeat pie is a festive dish and is often associated with Christmas. Like eggnog, it is sometimes considerably spiked with spirits. I suspect that applejack is often used, but most recipes list brandy or cognac—even rum and Madeira. Most of the recipes make large batches, and mincemeat is usually put up in sterile jars. The recipe below, which I have rather freely adapted from *Larousse Gastronomique,* is for a relatively small batch, and I recommend it highly. Be warned, however, that it *does* contain lots of good cheer.

The Mincemeat
1 pound boiled venison
1 pound beef suet
1 pound minced raisins
1 pound currants
1 pound tart apples, peeled and chopped
5 ounces candied citron, finely diced
3½ ounces candied orange peel, chopped
juice and chopped rind of an orange
1 pound light brown sugar
1 ounce mixed spices (cinnamon, mace, cloves, nutmeg)
2½ teaspoons salt
2 cups brandy
½ cup rum
½ cup Madeira

Grind the cooked venison, beef suet, and apples in meat grinder with a coarse blade. Put all the ingredients into a large bowl and mix thoroughly. Cover the bowl and put it into the refrigerator for a month. Stir the mixture every eight days.

Note: The mincemeat in this recipe is not cooked, except for the venison. Most American texts call for cooking the mixture. Also note that the measures will fill more than one pie of ordinary size.

The Pie
pastry for a 9-inch double pie crust
2 cups venison mincemeat
1 lemon

Preheat the oven to 450 degrees. Line a pie plate with pastry. Add the zest and juice of a lemon to 2 cups of venison mincemeat. Fill the pie and cover with the upper crust. Punch holes in it with a fork. Bake for about 30 minutes, or until the crust is browned.

If you have the knack, make your own pastry and try making small individual pies or tarts. The famous Banbury tarts of England are filled with a mixture quite similar to mincemeat.

Pie Pastry

Some of the best recipes for pie pastry call for lard (hog fat), an ingredient that may not be a staple in most modern households and may be a no-no for people with cholesterol concerns. Vegetable oil or shortening is usually recommended these days. Further, some of the old reliable recipes make a large batch of dough, whereas the modern cook might need only enough for one pie. Reducing the recipe doesn't always work, and besides, it's difficult to calculate and measure out exactly $7/32$ of a cup. Besides all this, making a good pie pastry is something of an art, and the truly accomplished practitioner uses a recipe only as a guide, knowing somehow that the present batch of flour, perhaps influenced by the humidity, is different from the last batch. All things considered, it is very tempting to purchase a frozen pie crust at the supermarket, complete in an aluminum baking pan.

ELEVEN

Cured Venison and Sausage

Salt has played a very important role in human history. More than any other substance, it has enabled man to preserve large quantities of fish and meat for future use. Although just about everybody in the United States and Canada has electricity for cooling and freezing meats these days, not long ago, salt pork, beef, and fish were the staples. Also, venison hams were salt cured and smoked exactly like pork hams, and salt-cured and smoked bear hams were, and are, considered to be choice eating in parts of Russia.

Early man also made use of other substances for preserving meat, including lard or other rendered fat. In this case, the meat was immersed in the fat and kept in a cool place. Honey and waxes were other well-known preservatives and can still be used today if needed.

Meat also has been canned, dried, and smoked by primitive peoples. Freezing was possible in some areas. For example, *giviak*, a great delicacy in Greenland, was made by stuffing various arctic birds into seal skins, which contained plenty of blubber, and freezing them under the ice. The *giviak* was often eaten raw in a partly frozen state.

Some of the old ways of curing and preserving meat are discussed in this chapter, along with modern methods of achieving similar effects. Remember that cured meat has a flavor unlike fresh meat, so culinary considerations are important. The patio cook who adds hickory chips to the coals of a grill isn't doing so to preserve meat. He is after flavor.

JERKY, DRIED VENISON, AND PEMMICAN

The American Indians and early settlers made full use of deer, buffalo, and other game by cutting the meat into strips and drying it in the open air. The dried meat was usually soaked in water before it was cooked, or else it was simmered in stews for a long time. It was also ground or pulverized. The old ways are still available to the American hunter, and I strongly recommend that anyone try making jerky on a clothesline or at least inside a screened-in porch. But modern electric and gas kitchen ranges can also be used; some people even make jerky in a microwave oven these days! In any case, jerky can be used while camping or backpacking, or it can be eaten as a snack. Anyone who has priced jerky at the market will surely want to try the recipes below.

I prefer my jerky to be on the chewy side. The meat is traditionally cut into small, narrow strips, with the grain. If it is cut against the grain, the strips tend to break into pieces. Of course, the meat should be cut against the grain if a crunchy texture is desirable, as when it is to be ground and used in pemmican or other recipes.

Green River Clothesline Jerky

Here's a recipe from *Cooking in Wyoming,* submitted by Eunice Hutton of Green River, who says that she got it years earlier from her mother, who in turn got it from a Mr. Payne, an early resident of Green River. The recipe specified elk meat, but it will work with other good venison.

> 3 or 4 pounds venison, cut into long, thin strips
> salt and water
> 1 cup brown sugar
> 1 tablespoon allspice (crushed)
> 1 tablespoon saltpeter (potassium nitrate)
> ½ tablespoon red pepper flakes

Put a layer of venison into an oblong glass container and top with a thin layer of salt. Continue the layers until all the venison is

132

used. Melt the brown sugar in some water and mix in the crushed allspice, saltpeter, and red pepper. Pour the mixture over the meat and let it soak for 36 hours. Then, as Ms. Hutton said, "Take a large darning needle with twine and make a loop on each piece of meat, string on a wire or hang up with a clothes pin." The meat should hang for several days or until dry. This recipe works best on cool, dry, sunny days.

Smoked Venison Jerky

Cut the venison into strips about 1 inch wide, ⅜ inch thick, and 7 inches long (or just long enough to fit into a storage jar). Rub the strips with salt and black pepper, then leave them on a rack in a cool, dry place for a day or two. Next, put the jerky into a smoker and cold smoke it for several hours. A silo-shaped water smoker without water in the pan will do, but a cold smoker works best. After smoking, store the meat in a glass "fruit jar."

Oven Jerky

It's possible to make some very good jerky in the kitchen oven, if the temperature is held to low. Here's a good recipe.

> 3 pounds venison strips
> ½ cup soy sauce
> ½ cup Worcestershire sauce
> juice of 1 lemon
> 1 teaspoon black pepper
> 1 teaspoon salt
> 1 teaspoon Liquid Smoke (optional)

Cut the venison into strips ¼ to ⅜ inch thick. Put the meat and other ingredients into a glass container and marinate overnight. Drape the strips onto the racks of an oven with a drip pan at the very bottom. Set the oven at 150 degrees or lower. Bake for 6 to 8 hours, or until the jerky is dry. Remember, however, that the thermostats on some ovens are not accurate, so be sure to check the jerky on the hour to make sure that it doesn't char.

Microwave Jerky

If you're in a hurry, try the above recipe in a microwave. Partly freeze the meat, then cut it into slices about ⅛ inch thick. Zap it on high for 3 minutes, then zap and check in 30-second periods until the meat is dry to your satisfaction. Most microwaves are small and the strips should be spread out, so only a small amount can be made at a time.

Dried Venison Meat Loaf

Here's another old Western recipe that I have adapted from *Cooking in Wyoming*, to which it was submitted by Stella Maestas of Rawlins. As the book said, "This recipe has been passed down through the generations from Mrs. Maestas' great-grandmother in New Mexico, Mrs. Dessie Romero, to all the members of her family." The book then said to slice the meat when fresh and hang it on a line to dry. Presumably it contained no salt or spices. When dry, it was stored until needed for cooking. Such dried meat could be soaked in water overnight and then cooked with various recipes, or merely put into a suitable soak, as in the Maestas recipe, which says to grind 3 pounds of dried venison, then mix it with 1 cup raisins, 2 teaspoons cinnamon, and 1 teaspoon cloves. Then, caramelize 1 cup white sugar in a heavy skillet. When brown, add 3 cups hot water and boil until sugar dissolves. Mix boiling liquid with meat mixture and let stand to cool. Put mixture into cheesecloth sack. Place a heavy weight on it and let it drain until dry. Slice like meat loaf to eat.

Pemmican

American Indians made a high-energy trail food from meat that had been dried (as in making jerky), ground, and mixed with bear fat and dried berries. Blueberries, buffalo berries, and many others were used, depending on location and availability. The mix was carried on hunting trips in leather pouches and was also stored and eaten during the winter months when other food might be scarce.

Anyone who wants to try pemmican should first make some jerky and grind it or beat it so that it can be mixed well with fat.

Any good fat that doesn't require refrigeration can be used. Try Crisco. Mix equal parts (by weight) of ground meat, fat, and dried berries. Shape the mixture into thumb-sized pieces. Modern Indians can wrap each piece in plastic film. For long storage without refrigeration, it's best to dip the pieces in melted paraffin and keep them in a cool place.

American settlers picked up the pemmican idea from the Indians, and no doubt added other ingredients. The mix itself became more widely used in recipes. In fact, it could be argued that the American version of mincemeat pie developed from pemmican, since most of the recipes call for ground meat (venison or beef), fat, and fruits. (See the recipe for mincemeat pie in chapter 10.)

Backpacker's Chili

Put some jerky into a container and cover it with water. Add a little chili powder and simmer for several hours, or until the jerky is tender. If you're in a hurry or have dentures, pound the venison before cooking and make a chili soup.

VENISON SAUSAGE

Essentially, sausage is nothing more than ground meat and seasonings stuffed into a casing, which is usually made from the intestine of a mammal. It's a very old method of packaging meat, and today it's much easier to make sausage from venison if you purchase salt-cured and dried casings from a meat processor or supplier. You'll need a meat grinder, a sausage stuffer, casings, seasonings, and other ingredients. These topics are discussed below.

Meat Grinders: Most home kitchens don't have a large electric grinder like the ones used by the professionals, but most any good grinder will do. There are some relatively inexpensive electric grinders and I recommend them if their primary purpose is to grind meat. Food processors and other multipurpose machines can be used, but the results are inconsistent and the meat may be too mushy, too lumpy, or both. I normally use an old hand-cranked meat grinder, the kind that clamps onto a tabletop. Some of the larger and more expensive hand-cranked models have four legs and have to be bolted down, which requires that holes be drilled in the table or countertop. So, if you are buying a new grinder, be sure that you can mount it before you pay.

Also be sure that you can obtain new cutting plates and other parts either from your dealer or directly from the manufacturer. The plates have a number of sharp-edged holes that actually cut the meat and extrude it. If you grind lots of meat and other foods, the plates will become dull and should be replaced. Usually, I use a plate with ³⁄₁₆-inch holes, but other sizes come in handy from time to time. Often I'll grind the meat first with a ⅜-inch plate, then switch to a ³⁄₁₆-inch size.

Also, any unit that you purchase should have tube attachments or several attachments of various sizes for use in stuffing sausage. (Stuffers are discussed later.) These tubes should be available from the dealer or directly from the manufacturer.

A good meat grinder will come in handy for making any sort of ground meat and other ground foods, such as mincemeat, hamburger, or gameburger. In my opinion, it is always better to grind your hamburger or gameburger shortly before cooking. Venison and other meats freeze better in chunks than in ground form, and, as explained in the section on ground meat, the beef or pork fat can be put in or left out, depending on how the ground meat is to be cooked. Also, having a grinder at home permits you to experiment with mixes of meat, such as venison and lean pork or turtle. If you like really good ground meat, as I do, you may find yourself buying chunks of beef, pork, and lamb and grinding it at home. That way, you'll have more control of the fat and tissue content and you'll have a fresher grind. It may also be cheaper to buy meat from the butcher in larger chunks.

Sausage Stuffers: There are several types of stuffers, all of which have a tube over which the casing fits. In some of the larger stuffers, the sausage mixture is forced into the casing by the action of a lever or screw pressure mechanism. Some of these are large-capacity units, are relatively expensive, and have to be bolted down. The more expensive stuffers are made from stainless steel; the others are made from tinned cast iron.

The best bet, at least for the beginner, is to purchase a grinder that has a tube stuffer attachment, but even this is not necessary if you can rig some sort of funnel. The meat can be forced through by hand and into the casing, which is attached to the end of the funnel. Usually, the casing is twisted from time to time so that the sausages can be separated into convenient lengths. Sometimes air bubbles will form inside the casings, and these can be relieved by pricking the casing over the bubble.

Casings: At one time, farmers and others who butchered animals made their own casings by cleaning out the intestines. These days, it's easier to purchase casings from a meat processor or from a supplier for the meat business. These casings, often sold in hanks, are salt-cured and will keep for quite some time under refrigeration. They should be rinsed and soaked in water before use.

Casings are available from sheep, hogs, and cows, usually in several sizes from each type of animal. Ordinary stuffed sausage is usually made from casings in sizes from 32mm to 38mm and, for the beginner, I would recommend those in the 32mm to 35mm range. These will fit most stuffing tubes. (The tubes are tapered.) Smaller sheep casings can be used for making wieners, and large beef bungs can be used for bologna and such. Even hog stomachs, cleaned and salted, are available for making headcheese or souse.

In addition, synthetic casings are available.

Seasonings and Other Ingredients: All you really need to make good sausage is a mix of salt, pepper, and perhaps a little sage. But all manner of spices, herbs, and other ingredients can be used, depending on the recipe and the kind of sausage you are making. Polish sausage has different seasonings than pepperoni and chorizo, and blood sausage will need fillers such as buckwheat groats. Anyone who is seriously interested in sausage should buy a good book on the subject and look at some catalogs from various suppliers. The seasonings can be mixed as needed, or if you are going to make lots of one kind of sausage, a seasoning mix can be made at home. Also available are kits that contain packets of seasonings and cures as well as casings.

Sausage Cures: If you are going to smoke, cure, or dry sausage, you must use a proper cure to help prevent botulism. There are several mixes on the market, but saltpeter (potassium nitrate) is one of the more common cures. Sea salt contains some potassium nitrate, but this is removed from most table salt these days. Salt-peter also helps keep the meat a nice pink color.

For all sausage that is to be smoked or dried, I use a mix suggested by Jack Ubaldi in his *Meat Book:* 4 pounds salt, 1 pound sugar, and 1¼ ounces of saltpeter. This mixture can be kept in a jar and used as needed. Usually, 2½ tablespoons of the mixture should be added to each 3 pounds of meat. Of course, the mix can be ground into the meat, along with pepper, sage, and other flavorings. If you don't want to go with this basic mix, start with the recipes below.

Old-Timey Smoked Sausage

Here's a recipe that I ran across in *Cracklin Bread and Asfidity*, a book written by Jack and Olivia Solomon, old friends of mine. It is obviously for use in a smokehouse, such as the one that stood behind my house when I was a boy. I remember my father smoking sausage, and he always used green hickory. Green wood, of course, makes a lot of smoke and doesn't burn as quickly as dry wood, so that you didn't have to get up at all hours of the night to add fuel to the fire. Anyhow, this recipe was contributed by Mrs. George Moreman, and I have changed the meat from "lean pork with some fat" to "venison with some fat pork."

>   8 pounds venison with some fat pork
>   3 tablespoons sea salt (see note)
>   2 tablespoons black pepper
>   2 tablespoons sage

"Measure and mix seasonings. Sprinkle over ground pork [and venison], mix thoroughly with hands. Can be ground the second time for a finer grade of sausage. Stuff in casings with sausage grinder stuffer. When they are stuffed, hang over about 3-inch hickory poles and put a smoke from green hickory chips under sausage to smoke two or three days. Poles should be at least 5 feet above the smoker."

Note: Remember that some old recipes such as the one above use salt that would, at the time, be likely to contain some saltpeter and other preservatives. These days, most of these minerals are removed from table salt before it is packaged for sale in the supermarket.

Easy Sausage

Everyone who makes sausage frequently will have a secret ingredient or two, one spice or another, making it the world's best. The beginner can get by with a mix of spices and seasonings from specialty suppliers. Be sure to read the directions on the package before using the seasoning so that the ratio of meats can be adjusted. Usually, 12 pounds of combined sausage meats or fat will require a 4-ounce package of seasoning.

> 9 or 10 pounds venison
> 2 or 3 pounds beef suet or fatty pork
> prepared seasonings

Cut the meat and suet into chunks and mix it together, along with the seasonings. This works best if you first cube the venison and spread it out on a table or counter. Then cut the fat and spread it out atop the venison. Next, sprinkle the seasonings over everything. Mix the meats and run through a grinder using a coarse plate, then run the mixture through using a smaller plate. This sausage can be used as patties or stuffed into casings. The links can be used fresh or smoked/cooked to an internal temperature of at least 140 degrees. If the sausage is to be dried or cold smoked, some saltpeter should be added to the seasonings.

Venison and Pork Sausage

One of my favorite low-fat recipes for venison sausage was published in *The Official Louisiana Seafood & Wild Game Cookbook:* "Take about 15 pounds of lean venison with absolutely no fat on it at all. Venison fat is strong and musky and not good eating. Use the same amount of lean, fresh pork as you have of venison. [Yes, some cuts of pork are quite lean.] Your mixture should be half and half to be really good. Grind up the meats and mix them together thoroughly.

Then add 4 ounces of water, mixing well. Now mix in your seasonings: 1½ ounces of red pepper, 1 ounce of nutmeg, ½ ounce of paprika, 2 teaspoons of garlic powder, 12 ounces of salt, and ½ pound of dried milk. At this point it is a good idea to cook a little of the sausage mixture and adjust seasonings to your particular taste. Stuff the meat in casings, keeping the links about 6 to 8 inches long. The meat may also be molded into patties and wrapped in aluminum foil."

Venison Sausage and Barley

This is one of my favorite recipes for venison sausages as well as barley. It should be cooked in a large skillet that has a lid. A stove-top Dutch oven will do.

> 1 pound smoked venison sausage
> 1 cup pearl barley
> 4 cups chicken stock or bouillon broth
> 1 medium-to-large onion, chopped
> 2 tablespoons cooking oil or margarine
> 1 tablespoon chopped parsley (½ tablespoon dried)

Cut the sausage links into ½-inch wheels and brown slightly in a skillet with the cooking oil. Remove the sausage and sauté the chopped onions, parsley, and barley for a few minutes. Stir in the stock or bouillon and bring to a boil. Add sausage. Cover tightly, reduce heat, and simmer for 40 minutes, until the barley absorbs the moisture. It's best to check the dish from time to time to see whether a little water is needed. If there is too much moisture after 40 minutes, simmer uncovered for a few additional minutes. Garnish with a sprig or two of fresh parsley. This dish makes a satisfying hot lunch on a cold day.

CORNED VENISON

Originally, corning was a method of preserving or pickling meats and can still be used for this purpose, especially in conjunction with modern refrigeration. Corning venison for immediate use (for flavor) was discussed in the recipes for corned venison and cabbage and New England boiled dinner in chapter 7. The method given in that chapter used only salt. Recipes for longer preservation call for sodium nitrate, sodium nitrite, or saltpeter, all of which are available at the pharmacy. A ready-mixed pickling cure, such as Morton Quick, can be used. These are available at some supermarkets, and have pickling directions on the package. Most people put other ingredients into the corning brine for flavor.

This recipe has been adapted from "Cooking the Sportsmen's Harvest II," published by the South Dakota Department of Game, Fish, and Parks. It makes about 2 gallons of pickling solution, which is plenty for corning 8 to 10 pounds of venison, or two rump roasts.

> 1½ cups table salt
> ½ cup brown sugar
> 1 medium onion, sliced
> 1 medium lemon, sliced
> 1 clove garlic, minced
> 2 tablespoons pickling spice mix
> 1 teaspoon peppercorns
> 3 teaspoons sodium nitrate
> 1 teaspoon sodium nitrite
> 1 teaspoon cloves
> 3 bay leaves
> 7 quarts warm water

Mix all the dry ingredients well and put them into a large crockery or other non-metallic container. Stir in the water, then add the onion, garlic, and lemon. Add the meat, which should be submerged. It may help to put a plate bottom-down on top of the meat, then weight the plate. Put the container in a cool place for 15 days, turning the meat every day or two.

When you are ready, rinse the meat and cook it by any corned beef recipe, or try the recipes in chapter 7.

TWELVE

Venison for Breakfast

When she isn't on a diet, my good wife can make the best country-fried venison steak breakfast that I ever tasted. It seems especially fitting whenever one of my boys brings home a deer, and with it we feed the family and perhaps a spend-the-night teenager or two. This is always a good time for all.

Helen's Venison Breakfast

Unfortunately, my wife doesn't have rigid measures to follow, but the ingredients are quite simple. One key to the recipe is in having good meat and not overcooking it. Whether they need it or not, she always beats the steaks with the edge of a plate or saucer or, sometimes, with the mouth of a jar. When using the plate, she beats the meat first one way and then the other, in a crisscross pattern. Then she salts and peppers each piece and dredges it in flour. Next, she cooks it over medium heat in a heavy skillet in about ½ inch of peanut oil until it is nicely browned. This steak should not be cooked too long; when cut, it should show a little red juice.

At just the right time, she takes the steaks out of the skillet, puts them on a heated platter, and starts another batch. When all the steaks are done, she pours off most of the oil and scrapes the bottom of the skillet with a wooden spatula. Next, she mixes a little flour and water and pours some very slowly into the skillet, stirring constantly, until a thick gravy forms.

Meanwhile, she will have mixed biscuit dough and preheated the oven. While the biscuits are baking, she puts the platter of steaks atop the oven to stay warm. When the biscuits are nicely browned on top, we're ready to eat. Now it's every man for himself, and we usually put two or three pieces of steak on one side of the plate and two biscuit halves, soft part up, on the other side. The gravy is spooned over all of it, and elbows are put on either side of the plate as we hunker down to the business at hand, unless we've got snooty guests in the house. I confess that I sometimes prepare this meal, but somehow it doesn't always come out quite the same. Normally, I make the gravy a little differently, in that I pour off the excess grease and then put a little flour into the bottom of the skillet and cook it, as when making a roux. Then I add a little water, stirring slowly, until the gravy forms. Usually this works.

I might point out that country-fried steak is sometimes quite tough, especially if a piece of venison is cooked for too long. If in doubt, cut off a piece of steak before serving it. If this piece chews like rubber, all is not lost. Simply add a little more water to the gravy, return the steaks to the skillet, sprinkle on a little more pepper, and simmer it for 1 hour, or until tender, turning from time to time and adding more water as needed. The steak gets better as it cooks.

Although I consider country-fried venison steaks to be the best possible American breakfast, I do enjoy a different menu from time to time, such as a little venison liver sautéed with butter and onions. Also, venison sausage always goes well with eggs.

Venison Hash

This dish is made with leftover or boiled venison. I like it for a hearty breakfast, along with biscuits and black coffee.

> 2 cups chopped venison (precooked)
> 4 medium potatoes
> 2 medium onions
> 1 medium tomato
> 1 cup of water and a bouillon cube
> ¼ cup bacon drippings or cooking oil
> salt and pepper to taste

Dissolve the bouillon cube in a cup of hot water. Finely dice the potatoes, onions, and tomato. Heat the bacon drippings or oil in a heavy skillet with a cover. Stir-fry the diced potatoes, onions, and tomato on high heat for a few minutes. Add the bouillon and cook on high until the mixture is quite hot. Reduce heat, cover, and cook very slowly for 20 minutes. Add the chopped venison, salt, and pepper. Increase heat and stir. Serve when the venison is heated through.

Eggs and Venison Brains

This is one of my favorite dishes, and I usually scramble it on the stove top in a skillet. My wife, on the other hand, prefers to bake it in the oven. Also, some folks insist on putting a little milk into the mixture. Suit yourself.

> chicken eggs
> venison brains
> green onions with tops
> butter
> salt and pepper

The proportions for this recipe aren't exact, but I like to keep the eggs and brains in more or less equal amounts by volume. I also allow one green onion with about half the top per *large* egg or for two small eggs. Break the eggs into a bowl and whisk in the brains and chopped green onions. Heat a little butter in a skillet and scramble the mixture until firm. Salt and pepper to taste. Serve with buttered toast.

Alaskan Scrapple

As the name implies, scrapple was made from scraps of meat (originally pork) left from home or farm butchering. The dish is said to have originated in Colonial Philadelphia. It is very good and can be made from venison and other meat, as shown in the recipe below from *Alaska Magazine's Cabin Cookbook:*

> Use scrap or shoulder meat of any big game. Cover meat with water and cook until tender, adding an onion for extra

flavor. Drain off the liquid and measure. Grind the meat. Use 1½ quarts broth for each quart of meat. Add water to the broth if necessary to make the required amount. Put the broth in a large saucepan over high heat. Stir in 1 cup of cornmeal for each quart of liquid. Sprinkle it on the boiling broth by hand to avoid lumping. Reduce the heat to low and simmer for half an hour. Add the ground meat and season with salt and pepper. A wooden spoon should be used for stirring this concoction. Simmer the mixture until it is quite thick.

Pour into loaf pans to cool and harden. To serve, slice thinly, roll in flour, and fry until lightly browned on both sides. Serve hot with syrup and butter, too, if desired.

The original Philadelphia recipe included a little sage, and was served for breakfast with maple syrup.

Venison Sausage for Breakfast

I've always been fond of smoked link sausage for breakfast. Sometimes I broil the links in the oven until I think they're done. More often, I cut the sausage into ½-inch wheels and steam for about 10 minutes in an electric skillet with a lid. This can be served with eggs or other breakfast fare.

I also sometimes make sausage patties for breakfast, using venison and bacon ground together, as follows.

2 pounds venison
½ pound bacon
1 teaspoon salt
1 teaspoon pepper
½ teaspoon sage

Chop the bacon and dice the venison, then mix in the salt, pepper, and sage. Refrigerate the mixture for a few hours before use. Shape the mixture into thin patties. Pour a little oil into a skillet or onto a griddle (or use no-stick spray) and heat to medium high. Grill the patties for a few minutes on each side. Serve with scrambled eggs and toast.

Note: Any sort of fatty pork can be used in this recipe. You can try a tablespoon of canola or peanut oil mixed with the meat, but bacon or salt pork has better flavor.

Also, remember that either smoked link sausage or sausage patties go well with other breakfast combinations. In my native South, many people eat sausage for breakfast along with grits and even with biscuits and syrup, or cornbread and syrup. I'll eat any of these, but I really prefer to put a hot venison sausage patty between biscuit halves and eat it like a sandwich.

THIRTEEN

Marinades and Sauces

Anyone looking herein for long sauce and marinade recipes and such has got the wrong book. Usually, when a marinade is required, I try to make it an integral part of the recipe instead of sending the reader off to other pages. Not all of the recipes call for marinades, however, and here and there, I might direct the reader to marinate at will, depending, I would hope, on the quality of the meat or the chef's perception of it. Some people automatically hold that all venison is "gamy" and should be soaked for three days in vinegar, in which case it will taste like vinegar, not good venison. On the other hand, there are indeed some good recipes that call for marinades that considerably influence the flavor of the meat, as in sauerbraten. For the most part, however, good venison requires no more marinade than good beef.

MARINADES

I sometimes like to marinate venison in red wine or wine vinegar for 10 or 12 hours before cooking. "Marinate with" might be more correct. The liquid doesn't have to cover the meat, so wine vinegar merely sprinkled onto the meat will sometimes do. Usually, such marinated meat will be in bulk, so that tossing it from time to time will help coat it nicely.

For a quicker marinade, I sometimes sprinkle venison slices or chunks heavily with Dale's steak seasoning, lemon juice, onion juice, or zesty Italian salad dressing. Pineapple juice is a quick tenderizer.

Still, marinating isn't a cure-all for venison that has not been properly killed, field dressed, and hung, as I said at the outset. A deer that has been chased all over the country by dogs, killed and tied across the hood of a Jeep, and driven through town hours after the kill is not fit for human consumption and marinating won't help. On the other hand, prime venison is one of the very best of meats and requires no marinating in order to be choice eating. But most cooks will want to marinate meat from time to time, and I recommend the following recipes.

Arm and Hammer Marinade

I sometimes marinate tough meat, or meat that smells a little off to me, with the following:

> 1 tablespoon baking soda
> 1 quart of water

Mix the marinade and pour it over the meat in a non-metallic container. The baking soda will impart a clean color to the meat and often take away the smell, up to a point. Venison ought to smell like venison, just as fish should smell like fish. As a rule, stew meat or small chunks should soak in this marinade overnight. Roasts and other larger pieces should soak for two days or longer, under refrigeration.

Oriental Soak and Baste

This recipe can be used to marinate meat and baste it while grilling or broiling. I also like it to marinate meat that is to be fried.

> ½ cup peanut or olive oil
> ¼ cup soy sauce
> ¼ cup teriyaki sauce
> ¼ cup sherry or sake
> 2 tablespoons Worcestershire sauce
> fresh ginger (optional)
> 1 clove garlic, crushed

Mix all ingredients. When the mixture is to be used as a marinade, put the venison into a glass container, pour the mixture over it, and refrigerate overnight. The leftover marinade, or a fresh batch, can also be used as a basting sauce for grilled or broiled venison. I have also used it as a "stir-fry" marinade. If you've got fresh ginger, put a couple of slices into the marinade.

A.D.'s Favorite Marinade

cow's milk

That's right. Merely cover the meat with fresh, whole milk and soak it overnight. This mild marinade is especially useful for stew meat. In camp, one can mix powdered milk or even powdered buttermilk, but fresh is better, at least to me. I suppose that fresh goat's milk or yak milk would do just as well, but I'm not sure.

SAUCES

My recipes for sauces tend to be a little longer than those for marinades. Again, most of my sauces are tied to particular recipes and are treated as needed in other chapters. Here are a few others to consider.

Red Meat Sauce

This sauce goes nicely with venison and other game. I like it with any roasted or grilled meat.

> ½ cup catsup
> ½ cup red currant jelly
> ½ cup port
> 1 tablespoon butter
> 1 tablespoon Worcestershire sauce

Heat a small pan and add all the ingredients. Stir the ingredients on low heat until the jelly melts.

Venison Sauce Poivrade

This pepper sauce has a wonderful flavor that goes nicely with broiled or grilled venison. The peppercorns can be ground in a mill on a coarse setting, or can be crushed with a mortar and pestle.

> 1 can brown gravy (or thick brown sauce)
> 1 cup red wine vinegar
> 15 peppercorns, crushed
> ¼ cup red currant jelly

Mix the vinegar and pepper and simmer uncovered until the volume is reduced by half. Add the gravy and simmer for ½ hour, then stir in the jelly. Serve warm.

Wine Sauce for Venison

This recipe is made with 2 cups of stock, which can be from boiled venison or beef. If no stock is available and you don't choose to make your own, use water and bouillon cubes.

> 5 tablespoons butter
> 5 tablespoons flour
> 2 cups beef or venison stock
> ½ cup Madeira or port
> ½ cup red currant jelly

In a skillet or saucepan, melt the butter and stir in the flour, heating and stirring until the mixture browns, as when making a dark roux. Add the stock and bring to a boil. Add the wine and jelly and stir until the jelly blends with the sauce. Serve hot on sliced roast or boiled venison.

African Hot Sauce

In Mozambique, where grilling is a popular method of cooking meat, a combination marinade and sauce, *piripiri,* is made with hot red peppers. A similar sauce, *pili pili,* is made in Togo and other parts of West Africa. There are many variations, and the one below is made with butter and is intended to be served warm over grilled or broiled meat or to be used as a basting sauce when cooking kabobs. If you are after a hot marinade, omit the butter.

4 small red hot peppers
juice of 2 lemons
2 cloves garlic, crushed
1 cup butter
2 tablespoons minced parsley
¼ teaspoon sea salt

Melt the butter in a small saucepan. Juice the lemons. Crush the peppers and salt, and mince the parsley. Mix everything into the melted butter and simmer for about 20 minutes on low heat. Strain the sauce and brush it lightly over grilled or broiled meat. If you want to baste more liberally while cooking, increase the amount of butter.

Warning: This sauce is hot and can be dangerous, depending on the strength of your pepper.

Hot Stuff Barbecue Sauce

I have always like a hot barbecue sauce, and this recipe fills the bill. The hotness can be easily adjusted to suit your own taste by varying the amount of black pepper and Tabasco. Since the sauce isn't cooked, small, last-minute adjustments are easy.

1 small can tomato paste (6-ounce size)
1 cup cider vinegar
1 cup water
¼ cup Creole mustard
1 teaspoon salt
1 teaspoon black pepper
1 teaspoon Tabasco sauce

Mix all the ingredients well and keep at room temperature for several hours before using. Baste the venison during the last few minutes of cooking. If you feel that some sort of basting is required to keep the meat succulent during the cooking process, use vegetable oil or bacon drippings.

Maître d'Hotel Butter

This simple sauce requires no cooking and is served at room temperature. To make it, cream ½ cup butter and mix in 1 teaspoon salt, ¼ teaspoon white pepper, and 1 tablespoon finely chopped parsley. Then slowly stir in the juice of two lemons. This sauce goes nicely with grilled or broiled venison steaks or chops.

APPENDIX A

Ten Steps to Better Venison

As I tried to make clear in the Introduction, having a good venison recipe and knowing how to cook it guarantee nothing. The cook simply must have good meat to work with, no matter whether he is cooking beef, pork, or venison. Back when farmers butchered their own hogs instead of buying pork at the supermarket like the rest of us, they were careful to get them into a calm state of mind and then kill them cleanly and quickly. Something of an old joke was to "scratch a hog down." This meant that the farmer scratched the animal's back with a corncob, which apparently felt so good that the hog lay down to enjoy it and even went to sleep before the farmer struck. The deer hunter can't be quite so seductive, but certain steps can be taken (and mistakes avoided) that will surely lead to better venison.

1. Select a prime animal. Usually, a healthy animal will be plump and have a shiny coat. As a rule, a deer of either sex will make better eating before or after the rut, although this might well conflict with the best times to take an otherwise wary trophy. More often than not, a doe makes better eating than a buck and in my opinion, more hunters ought to take advantage of special doe seasons. Size, however, is not always a good indication of how good an animal will be as table fare. A fully mature deer is often just as good as a teenager.

In any case, if you want good meat, avoid shooting an animal that you think has been running. Many people who hunt with dogs, which is legal in some areas, don't want to hear all of this, but I'm saying it anyway. One of the worst things a hunter can do is to run a deer all over the country with dogs. In my part of the country, good ol' boys sometimes hunt in pickups or four-wheel-drive vehicles and communicate by CB radio. As often as not, the deer is shot from the truck as it crosses a road or even a highway. I am not judging this kind of hunting, provided it is done legally; I am speaking only in regard to good eating. Personally, I don't want a deer that was killed during the heat of the chase, although I believe that it is entirely possible to "drive" deer slowly for the sake of hunting without getting them too excited.

2. Choose a good stand. Where the hunter chooses to take his animal can be very important regarding the quality of the meat. Many whitetails are killed from tree stands, so that the hunter has control over location. But any stand or blind should be chosen in a spot that allows the hunter to identify the animal clearly and to get a clean shot. Further, when choosing a stand, the hunter should consider how he will get an animal out if he drops one.

If you are stalking or otherwise on the move, your location relative to transportation or a way out should always be a consideration. A good many moose have been shot in water, for example, and left because there was no way to get them out. As a rule, the choice of a stand often is more important in warmer areas of the country, at least from a culinary point of view.

3. Be a good hunter. Whoever shoots at a deer, or any other animal, should hit where he aims. The current consensus is that a lung shot is almost always the best bet. In addition to being a good marksman, he should also know the fundamentals of hunting. Wearing the right kind of clothes, for example, will often help the hunter get a better and a closer shot. In short, the cleaner the kill, the better the meat. Wounding a deer will happen from time to time, but the hunter should know that an animal dropped in its tracks will make better eating than one that runs for long distances after being shot.

4. Field dress the animal immediately. Unless you are in subzero weather, it is best to gut the animal and field dress it as soon as possible. This takes only a few minutes and can be accomplished on the ground instead of having to hang the animal. Start by inserting the point of a drop-point knife into the skin just behind the chest bone and opening it all the way to the rear. The rectum and urinary parts should be cut around and the tubes tied off, then pulled through the natural opening in the pelvic bone. (It is not necessary to cut the pelvic bone.) All this can be done with a knife that has a 3½- or 4-inch blade. The chest need not be cut open at this time, but the lungs and other parts should be removed by working the knife around the chest cavity and all the way to the neck. After all the innards are free, the deer should be rolled over on its side.

After the cavity has been voided, the deer can be moved over, out of the blood, and put on its belly to drain, with its legs pulled out. While the deer is draining, the hunter should sort out whatever innards he wants to keep. The liver of deer has no gallbladder, so that's not a worry. These parts are best put into a plastic bag and kept as cool as possible.

Next, turn the deer on its back. Prop the cavity open with sticks so that it will cool as rapidly as possible. The idea of quick field dressing is to cool the meat, not merely to remove the innards. This is accomplished in two ways: First, a good deal of the heat is removed with the innards; second, removing the innards creates an air pocket, and propping the cavity open will help air circulate inside.

At one time, bleeding the animal was standard practice, recommended by books and magazines on the subject. Generally, the animal's throat was cut and it was hung up to bleed, or propped up so that the head pointed downhill. This theory goes back to an old Arab method of slaughtering an animal, in which cutting the throat severed the jugular vein. This in turn resulted in quickly killing the animal (which was indeed important) but did not accomplish much bleeding, since the jugular goes only to the heart and the brain, not to the hindquarters where most of the meat is. It is possible to bleed the animal somewhat better by inserting the knife into the animal at the base of the chest and cutting in toward the heart, so that the large arteries going to the rear are cut. (This is sometimes called sticking.) But most people avoid this step these days, partly because the time is best spent in field dressing.

5. Move the meat. If you are going to keep the deer in camp for a few days, it's best to hang it in the shade. In warm weather, a game bag will be needed to keep flies away. In very cold weather, you need to prevent the animal from freezing at night and thawing during the day.

If you are on a one-day hunt, it's best to get the deer out of the woods as soon as possible. When taking it home or to the meat processor, don't let the meat get hot. Putting it across the hood of a truck is one of the worst things you can do, although it might show off the rack as you drive through town.

6. Age or freeze the meat. Either deliver the deer to a meat processor for aging or hang it at home, if you have a cool place. For best results, hang the deer for a week or two at 34 to 40 degrees. If possible, the temperature should remain constant. Be sure to avoid freezing the meat at night and allowing it to thaw out by day. If you don't have a meat processor on hand or don't choose to use one, and don't have a good place to hang the deer, it's best to skin the animal and cut it into quarters. These parts can be put into a large ice chest, or into more than one container if needed, and kept on ice for two weeks. This works best if you use a large chest with a drain hole. Dump ice in the bottom, put the meat inside, and cover it with more ice. Then close the cover and elevate the chest slightly on one end so that any water and blood will drain out. Add more ice from time to time, if needed.

If you can't hang the animal in a cool place, can't use a meat processor, and can't ice the meat down in chests, its best to skin the animal, butcher it immediately, and freeze it. If you have a refrigerator or a deep freezer, package the meat and start freezing it right away. Remember, however, that most home freezers can't chill a whole deer quickly, so it's best to freeze a few packages at a time. (Be sure to keep the rest of the meat in the refrigerator until you can transfer it to the freezer.) If the meat is properly butchered and packaged, venison that is frozen for several months without being hung is really quite good. Some people prefer to freeze fresh venison without hanging it, even if they have a choice, but some experts suggest that it be hung, which is my preference. In any case, proper aging not only improves the flavor of venison, but also makes it tender.

7. Butcher the meat according to how you plan to cook it. After hanging the carcass at a suitable temperature for about two weeks, skin it and butcher the meat as described above. I have discussed the various cuts in other chapters, so how you intend to cook the meat determines how you should butcher it. In a nutshell, I recommend that the roasts be boned, wrapped with freezer paper, labeled, and frozen. The hind leg should be reduced to a rump roast and ham. The ham should be further divided into small roasts, following the natural divisions between the muscles. These small roasts can be wrapped and frozen. Then they can be cooked whole as small roasts or sliced into chops.

I also recommend that scraps be trimmed and frozen as stew meat. In fact, it's not a bad idea to cut the whole deer up into stew meat, except perhaps for the loins and tenderloins. Then it can be thawed and cooked as such, or it can be ground into sausage or burger. If you want burgers to fry, add some fat as needed. If you want ground meat for spaghetti or other recipes, no fat will be required.

8. Preserve the meat. Not many people want to eat venison every day, so it's best to freeze or otherwise preserve some of the meat. Before freezing, wrap it in convenient units. I think that 1-pound packages (or small roasts) work best, for reasons given above. They also freeze and thaw more quickly than larger packages. Boning the meat reduces the volume to be fitted into your freezer, but keep the bones separately for soup, if possible.

If you don't have a freezer (or any space in it), you can pickle or corn the meat, or make jerky.

9. Choose the right recipe. For those of us who like to hunt and fish, the inclination is to cook a whole ham of venison or a whole 10-pound fish. Perhaps we have a need to show off, and yes, I think we should be proud of our hunting success. But I also feel that cooking and serving large chunks of meat is not the way to introduce some people to the wonderful world of fish and game cookery. As a rule, the larger the piece of meat, the harder it is to cook to perfection. And, as I have pointed out elsewhere, most people tend to cook venison too long simply because it is wild. Remember that most wild meat is already on the lean side, and tends to be comparatively tough, so that long, dry cooking adds to the problem.

For foolproof results, it is best to cook by a wet method, or with the aid of a crockpot, instead of baking or grilling it. Further, it is best to introduce newcomers to venison with recipes that have a familiar ring, such as venison stroganoff or Swiss steak.

10. Watch your manners. Avoid discussing "deer" or "moose" at the dining table. If a reference is necessary, use "venison," for the same reason that you usually say "pork" instead of "hog." This sort of talk doesn't bother me, and I confess that I have slanted the conversation to my advantage once or twice when the food was in short supply, but generally, fish and game should not be discussed at the table if you want your guests to enjoy your bounty.

Of course, it is always best to serve venison and other meats with the proper menu. Potatoes, green snap beans, mushrooms, and green salads are almost always in order, but many other foods and drinks can be served. Also remember that good company and conversation can add considerably to any meal, as does atmosphere, such as candlelight or a wood fire.

Once, my wife and I lived on an island in Lake Weir, Florida, and since the fishing was good, we seemed to have lots of company. Some stayed the night, and one visitor always brought us something good to eat, as if in payment. Once, he brought a gallon of venison chunks that he had grilled and smoked on a rig made from a 55-gallon drum. During and after cooking, he had soused the meat in lots of sauce, heavy on Worcestershire. It was good, and we started eating it with beer. I ate so much that I felt that I had to say, "Man, this is good deer meat," every time I reached for a piece. He, on the other hand, slowed down and finally quit eating altogether. Finally, he said, "A.D., I would appreciate it if you would call the stuff venison instead of deer meat."

This full-grown man, well primed with beer, couldn't even eat his own venison expertly prepared by his own hand with his favorite method of cooking! Imagine how he would have felt if *I* had cooked it.

APPENDIX B

Metric Conversion Tables

U.S. Standard measurements for cooking use ounces, pounds, pints, quarts, gallons, teaspoons, tablespoons, cups, and fractions thereof. The following tables enable those who use the metric system to easily convert the U.S. Standard measurements to metric.

Weights

U.S. Standard	Metric	U.S. Standard	Metric
.25 ounce	7.09 grams	11 ounces	312 grams
.50	14.17	12	340
.75	21.26	13	369
1	28.35	14	397
2	57	15	425
3	85	1 pound	454
4	113	2	907
5	142	2.2	1 kilogram
6	170	4.4	2
7	198	6.6	3
8	227	8.8	4
9	255	11.0	5
10	283		

Liquids

U.S. Standard	Metric	U.S. Standard	Metric
⅛ teaspoon	.61 milliliter	⅜ cup	90 milliliters
¼	1.23	½	120
½	2.50	⅔	160
¾	3.68	¾	180
1	4.90	⅞	210
2	10	1	240
1 tablespoon	15	2	480
2	30	3	720
¼ cup	60	4	960
⅓	80	5	1200

To convert	multiply	by
Ounces to milliliters	the ounces	30
Teaspoons to milliliters	the teaspoons	5
Tablespoons to milliliters	the tablespoons	15
Cups to liters	the cups	.24
Pints to liters	the pints	.47
Quarts to liters	the quarts	.95
Gallons to liters	the gallons	3.8
Ounces to grams	the ounces	28.35
Pounds to kilograms	the pounds	.45
Inches to centimeters	the inches	2.54

To convert Fahrenheit to Celsius: Subtract 32, multiply by 5, divide by 9.

Index

Notes

Notes